My Story
Faith, Family, Farm

Marjorie M. Beyersdorf

Green Bay, WI

My Story: Faith, Family, Farm by Marjorie M. Beyersdorf, copyright © 2017 by Marjorie M. Beyersdorf.

Marjorie M. Beyersdorf's author photo and other photos included in this book, courtesy of the Beyersdorf/Stanelle Family.

"The Old Tent" by Steve Coyle, © 2013 by Joni and Friends. Reprinted by permission of Joni and Friends.

"The Battle of My Gods" by Evan Stanelle, © 1995 by Evan Stanelle. Reprinted by permission of Evan Stanelle.

This book is a true story about the real life of Marjorie M. Beyersdorf of Wausau, Wisconsin. All names and locations are real. This book is about facts and actual events that happened to the author and her life's decisions. Written Dreams Publishing does not approve, condone or disapprove of the author's life decisions.

All rights reserved. In accordance with the U.S. Copyright Act of 1976, no part of this publication may be reproduced, distributed, or transmitted in any form or by any means, or stored in a database or retrieval system, without prior written permission of the publisher, Written Dreams Publishing, Green Bay, Wisconsin 54311. Please visit writtendreams.com to see more of the unique books published by Written Dreams Publishing.

Editor: Brittiany Koren

Copy-editor: Jessie Harrison

Cover art designer: Ed Vincent and Barbra Sprangers

Interior layout designer: Amanda Dix

Category: Christian Women's Memoir

Description: *Despite many hardships and losses, Marjorie M. Beyersdorf's trust in the Lord helped her through her life's trials on the farm.*

Large Print Hardcover ISBN: 978-0-9991870-5-0

Paperback ISBN: 978-0-09962521-7-1

Ebook ISBN: 978-0-9962521-9-5

Library of Congress Catalog Data: Applied for.

First Edition published by Written Dreams Publishing in August, 2017.

Green Bay, WI 54311

This book is dedicated to my children:

Robert Jr.

Kathryn Ann

Mary Ellen

Richard John

Lanetta May

Jeffery Joseph

Jeremy Jon

Introduction

We are born into life, not solely in control of our journey here on Earth. Little did I know what lie ahead on my pathway. Having become an orphan at the age of four…a child bride and parent at age fourteen…giving birth to seven children and having two of them taken away through death…going through two divorces…and operating the farm alone with two sons as a single parent…

At times, with tears in my eyes, I'd write about my experiences of the past. The insecurities and fears, being gullible, the weaknesses, blunders and failures, only to come to know that through it all, God's forgiveness and saving grace saved me from the lusts of the flesh and the pride of life.

As I look back, I know the definition of God's unconditional love, mercy, and grace. His Hand of Sovereignty and His strength were—and are—made perfect in my weakness.

We are made up of three people: the person that people know; the person we know ourselves; and the person God knows.

He knows me better than I know myself, and so I humbly wrote *My Story: Faith, Family, Farm*.

John Lingle and Hilda Stanelle on their wedding day with Aunt Norma Stanelle and Uncle Herman Weggan

Grandmother Ella Stanelle holding Marjorie and Grandfather Harry Stanelle with Richard, 1939

Beginnings Cut Short

A small house located at 205 West Seventh Street, Kaukauna, Wisconsin was to be the new address of John and Hilda (Stanelle) Lingle after their marriage on March 2, 1935. Before the year ended, my brother, Richard John was born, and I, Marjorie May, joined the family four years later, on March 27, 1939. Our home was one of a twin-duplex, located next to a corner vacant lot, which was to our east.

April 19, 1943 was a typical Monday morning. My brother, Richard had gone off to school at Park Elementary several blocks away. I was outside riding my tricycle, thinking about going and catching the little animals hidden out in the lot next door. A shrill bird call was sounding off from amongst the tall grasses and trees. The warmth of the sun shone on my face.

Mom was in the kitchen, and I could see her through the window. She was standing at the kitchen counter preparing lunch for Daddy to take to work. Daddy was in the house too, getting ready to go to work at the Thilmany Paper Mill, where he was a worker on the second shift.

After being outside for quite a while, I went into the house through the front door to get a drink of water. Daddy met me there, and pointed to a gun that was lying on the floor. He asked me to pick it up and take it upstairs for him. So I picked it up, resulting in the gun pointing through the archway and dining room, directly toward Mom. Reaching over my shoulder, he showed me how not to touch "this", meaning the trigger. But in doing so, he had his finger there and pulled it back, setting off the gun.

The noise from the gun scared me. And then, I suddenly saw Mom on the floor in a pool of blood. Being so very frightened, heart pounding, I screamed and wanted to run to her. What had just happened?

Daddy scooped me up into his arms, wiping my tears, and took me over to the next door neighbors'. Soon, other neighbors came, and policemen, too. Others came as well when they heard the shocking news of the tragedy in the Lingle home. Being very young, I didn't comprehend it all. It was as if an eclipse was appearing, and time stood still.

Later, as I grew older, I found out there had been an article in the local Kaukauna Times newspaper the following day with the headlines that read, *Husband Confesses to Shooting of His Wife*. The investigation, with questioning, took place over 26 hours, revealing what apparently seemed an accident, but turned out to be otherwise. It was planned to appear accidental. In reality, it was premeditated. I was instructed not to touch the trigger, but with my father's hand showing me, and ultimately pulling the trigger, he had killed my mother.

It was learned during the investigation that Daddy had gone to visit Mom's home place many times, where her younger sister was living, to see her without Mom's knowledge. On one such occasion, Sunday, April 18, my brother Richard (Dickie, as he was known then) went along with Daddy. Dickie had seen Aunt Letty and Daddy kissing in a very close embrace. He said he was going to tell Mom when they got home, but he didn't want to hurt her feelings. Daddy, knowing that his extra-marital affair would surface, became very nervous. He didn't want Mom to know he was involved with her sister. Thus, things happened quickly; my coming from the outside into the front door of our house, a gun conveniently laying on the floor, instructions for me to take the gun upstairs, and then, a moment of action affecting a lifetime.

John Lingle confessed and pleaded guilty to murder in the first degree for having shot his wife with a .22 caliber rifle in their home on April 19, 1943. He was sentenced to life imprisonment in the State Prison in Waupun, Wisconsin, exchanging his name for Number 27539.

I have some memory of Mom's funeral. A lot of people were giving me and Dickie a lot of attention. Specifically, I recall my Uncle Bert holding me at the cemetery. An airplane had flown overhead and held my attention until it disappeared out of sight.

My brother and I had become wards of the State. The Juvenile Judge placed us into the temporary custody of our maternal grandfather, Harry Stanelle. Several couples indicated interest in adoption, even to the point of separating us. However, our grandfather came forward and said he wouldn't take support funds, and wanted us raised as brother and sister. The

Juvenile Court appointed Grandfather as our permanent legal guardian. And so, what had been our family of four, with Mom, Dad, my brother, and I, was suddenly changed to a family of nine.

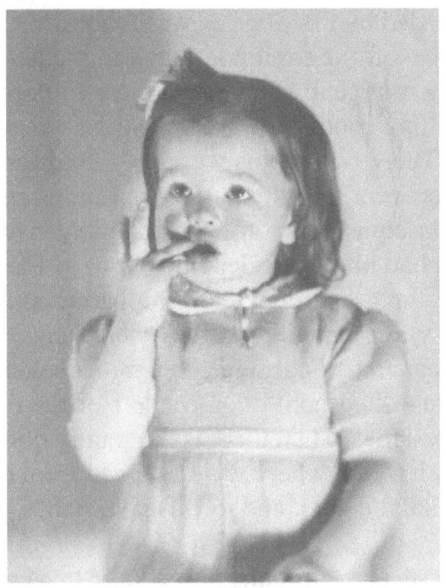

Marjorie May, age 2 years, 1941

My New Home

Grandmother had died a year earlier on February 6, 1942, but Grandfather wasn't alone in raising us. He had help. We had three uncles: Bert, Donald and Harry Jr., and three aunts: Norma, Selma and Letty. Aunt Norma took the role of surrogate mother. She made sure we had everything we needed and food to eat.

Grandfather owned the Stanelle Homestead, located one mile north of Forest Junction, WI and a quarter mile west of State Hwy 57. It was built in the 1870s by my great-grandfather, Gottlieb Stanelle. The house was immense, and I could easily get lost inside. It was also elegantly decorated.

The parlor had very attractive wallpaper, even on the ceiling, and the woodwork was carved with designs.

A long open porch bordered the north side of the house where, in summer, we would sit outside, and wash our feet in a foot pail. The pond was a short way off in the distance; and at eventide or the close of the day, we would be serenaded by the frogs as we scrubbed.

The entrance door, off the front porch and to the left, was the door that went into the sitting room and fancy parlor. Our Christmas tree was set up each year in the sitting room. A player piano was also kept there, which played roll music. These two rooms were only used for funerals of family members. We never went into the parlor, and only rarely into the sitting room, such as at Christmas time or when company visited.

The dining room had nine doors leading out of it. There was the hallway door, which led to three bedrooms and the bathroom. A closet door hid where dirty laundry and hanging clothes were kept. There was another door into the kitchen, and a door which led into a laundry room.

Grandfather's small bedroom door was off of the dining room, and it contained only necessities. Then there was a pantry door, and right next to it, a door to the wash room, where we'd come in from outside to hang our coats and caps behind the door, and to wash our hands. These made up the nine doors.

The upstairs had seven bedrooms, plus a large open room where several beds could be placed when needed. There was a unique room which was called a cupola, with a stairway leading up to the top of the house, where you could walk outside and see for a very far distance around the area. I was told this allowed the family to watch out for predators, or any trespassers coming by. A black, wrought iron fence enclosed the lookout for safety.

There was no indoor plumbing in Grandfather's house. Behind the house was a two-door outdoor toilet. There was also a tall hand pump outside, where we'd get our drinking water from every day; and inside, on the edge of the kitchen counter, was a smaller hand pump where water was used for filling the reservoir on the wood cook stove. One more small hand pump was used for washing our hands in the wash room. All the hand pumps drew their water from a very large cistern located in the basement of the house. Later on, faucets were put in, along with a flush toilet, but no hot water. Nope; no shower stalls back then! We were allowed to take a full bath in the bathtub every Saturday evening; otherwise, we just had sponge baths. (At present, the Stanelle Homestead has been elegantly restored and remodeled by my cousin, Jim Stanelle.)

Grandfather was the adult German Sunday school teacher at the Evangelical United Brethren Church in Forest Junction. We all went to Sunday school and worship service every Sunday morning. I was very timid at Sunday school. The teacher gave us crayons and a coloring book. She told a Bible story while we colored a picture of what she was telling us about.

There was a lot of attention given to me. Mom had always put big curls in my dark brown hair, and so Aunt Norma did the same, making sure I always looked pretty for Sunday school. One of the older men in church always called me Shirley Temple because of those curls.

Right from the start, while living with Grandfather, I slept with my Aunt Norma. When she would go to an evening meeting, I'd pull blankets over my head, regardless of how warm it was, because I was so afraid to be alone. The blankets were my security. I had a lot of fears and insecurities, with a lot of unanswered questions. As a result, I sucked my thumb, which became a chronic habit even into my elementary school years.

Marjorie May and Richard at the Stanelle Homestead, 1941

Stanelle Homestead, 1940s

School

With summer drawing to a close, the school season would soon begin. My brother, Dickie would be going off to school, leaving me behind. There were no kindergarten classes; no preschool back then. And so, Grandfather talked to the State Superintendent, inquiring as to whether or not I could go to school early. The answer came back yes, if the teacher felt comfortable about it. There would be a trial period to see if it worked out.

This made me very happy, because I wanted to be with my brother very much and go along with him to school.

Holmes School, named after Oliver Wendell Holmes, wasn't far from Grandfather's farm, less than a quarter of a mile. It was a one-room schoolhouse. From the one main door, we entered into the hall, where coats and jackets could be hung on hooks and boots were set in winter. There was a divided door for girls' and boys' clothes to be kept separate. The hallway door led into the large school room, and off to the northeast corner was a door giving access to a small library area.

With no indoor plumbing, there was an outdoor toilet facility adjacent to the woodshed—one for the girls and one for the boys. The seats were bare boards with a circular opening, and in winter, *burrrrrr!* To wash our hands, we used a basin of water and a soap dispenser, drying them with paper towels.

In nice weather, my brother and I would walk to school. During winter, when there was a lot of snowfall, the snowplow would make huge banks on the sides of the road. We'd climb up on top of the banks and walk on them to school. Some winters, the snow banks were so high we were able to touch the telephone wires! Many times, we'd walk home for lunch.

Our teacher had the fire started each morning before students arrived. The upper grade students were assigned tasks: to get water from a hand pump outside in front of the school to fill the water bubbler and the wash basin used for hand washing. They also had to empty the waste water from the pail beneath the basin. There were other duties, such as putting up and taking down the American flag each day, and sweeping the floor at days' end.

A large wood stove, with doors that opened on both sides, was in the main school room. In the wintertime, the boys would fill the wood box, always keeping it full. Snow pants and cotton long stockings would be hung on the stove's doors to dry.

As I continued to go to school, all was going well. I became the first preschooler in Forest Junction with regular attendance. Betty Schmelter was my first teacher. She was a very kind lady. She taught me the English alphabet, how to write numbers up to 100, and I did a lot of coloring. Miss Schmelter taught all eight grades, which amounted to only about 20 students. The following year, I became a first grader with another girl, Grace Hoyer. It was just the two of us through all eight grades.

Certain times stood out, especially during my elementary school years.

Christmas day was a special time when a program was held, with everyone taking part in the plays and recitations. How exciting it was to get the wooden planks out of the woodshed and set them up on cement blocks to make a stage! White bed sheets were strung on tight wire to make the draw curtains. After several weeks of practice, we were ready to perform for the parents and general audience. Bags of candy, nuts, and fruit were handed out at the close of the program, along with the students' exchange gifts. It was an enjoyable night for everyone.

I remember, too, Arbor Day in April. We wouldn't have regular classes, and instead we'd have a "clean-up day". The entire lawn and area around the school was raked, and a bonfire was made, where we roasted hot dogs and tasty marshmallows.

The years passed quietly and without incident. But when I was in 5th grade, I had both whooping cough and bronchitis. The doctor came from Kaukauna to see me to make home visits three times a week. I could hear him come up the steep stairway to my room where I was restricted to bed. He'd take my temperature and listen to my lungs. My throat was so sore, I could hardly swallow.

Penicillin had been recently developed for injection use in 1940, and lucky me, I was a recipient of it, receiving three shots a week in the bottom. I was absent from school more than a month, and our house was quarantined. No one could come to visit me, though I do remember receiving many, many get well cards from friends and family.

Another not-so-happy experience was when my right shoulder was broken while playing Kick the Can. All eight grades were out together at noon recess time, and one of the seventh graders, meaning to kick the can, missed, and kicked my shoulder instead. I had been holding the can on my toe like a football.

Marjorie M. Beyersdorf

Marjorie May and Grandfather Harry Stanelle, 1943   Richard and Marjorie, 1945

Daddy

Prisoners at Waupun State Prison that excelled in good character and conduct were asked to do jobs, and even drive a car for errands for the prison. Dad had a driver's license, and would drive a quarter mile past Grandfather's farm off Highway 57. He would make deliveries to the Green Bay Reformatory. Although he was never allowed to stop and see us, in letters he'd write to us he would say, "I'll be driving by on my way to Green Bay," on a given day.

After completing the sixth grade at the age of ten, June 23rd and 24th, 1949 stood out for me during my elementary school years when Grandfather received a phone call. The call on the 23rd informed us that our dad, John Lingle, had been in an accident on the job, and taken to the hospital.

Several men had been in a tunnel installing refrigeration equipment for the prison butcher shop. An acetylene torch ignited tar in the dead end tunnel, and all the crew ran out through the exit; all of them, that is, except Dad, who ran the opposite way into the tunnel, assumingly to save more men. He was rescued and taken to the hospital, suffering from intense inhalation of fumes from the fire.

On June 24th, 1949 at 4:30 PM, Dad died in the hospital. The last time I had seen him was on April 19th, 1943, when he held me close as he carried me over to the neighbors' house after the tragic shooting and the death of my mom. And now I'd see him at his funeral.

The song, "Abide with Me" will remain in my thoughts always as I remember the funeral at the Greenwood Funeral Home, where it played as background music during the service. The room was full of people. I was hesitant to go in and view the body, but I eventually did with Grandfather and Dickie. Looking at his body, he didn't seem like my dad. It was all very surreal to me.

Grandma Lingle said to me that day, "You made up for John."

Among my mementos are the actual papers of Dad's Moody Bible Institute of Chicago correspondence course, which was known as "The Scripture of Truth". The certificate of completion was dated January 22nd, 1948. It was such a joy to read, in my dad's own handwriting, his outlining of the many Bible verses relating to man's sin, that it was necessary to repent, to come back to God through the redemptive work of Jesus and receive His one-time sacrifice on the cross, shedding His blood to wash away our sins. As it says in Hebrews 9:22, "...without the shedding of blood there is no forgiveness of sins."

I believe, based on the Word of God and Dad's own handwriting, that he truly repented of his wrongdoing and was forgiven. What a great reunion it will be when we will be together again one day with our Savior, Jesus Christ our Lord!

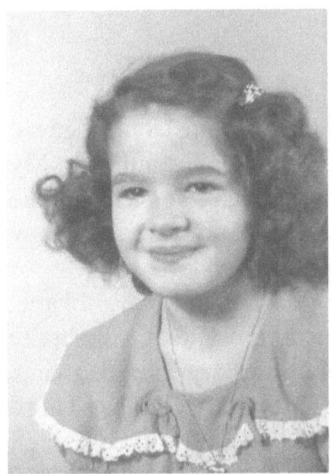

Marjorie May, 1947

Grandfather Harry Stanelle thrashing on the farm, 1947

Marjorie M. Beyersdorf

Marjorie May with Teddy the dog and Nicky the goat, her pets, on the Stanelle farm, 1948

Life on Grandfather's Farm

There were many animals on Grandfather's farm: about 18 milk cows, two teams of work horses, chickens for meat and eggs, and pigs. My brother and I had a pet goat named Nicky that was given to us. He and the farm dog, Teddy, were our companions. They were lots of fun, and many days, I did chores with both animals following me around the farm.

When I was older, Grandfather bought a small Shetland pony for me, which I named Silver. I grew to love animals a great deal, especially Silver. He was all mine. I'd hug him, and many times cry into his mane, knowing somehow, he understood my inner hurts and feelings. Those feelings of fear, insecurity, and aloneness haunted me daily, even though I was surrounded by aunts and uncles and a grandfather who loved me. I knew I wasn't *really alone*, but I could never stop feeling the sadness.

There was a lot of activity always going on at the farm. Grandfather planted a large vegetable garden every spring, and I'd get to be his helper. When the potatoes were planted, he'd make a hole. With my little pail of

My Story: Faith, Family, Farm

potatoes, I would put one in and he would cover it up. Then it was on to the next one. Later in the season, I'd help weed and thin out plants in rows.

Grandfather was the only one who owned a threshing machine in the local area, and he'd go from farm to farm, in customized work, cutting their grain and clover threshing. There would be about fifteen men, neighboring farmers who all worked together, to get it done.

When my uncle said I could hold the reins of the team of horses that pulled the wagon on which the bundles of grain were thrown, I was so excited! It was a great experience for me, even though my uncle stayed close by.

The neighbor wives would come together and make meals on whoever's farm they were at that day. They would serve meat, potatoes, vegetables, homemade bread, and pies—the whole works! All the food would be spread out on a large wooden table outside the house. Because it was usually very hot and humid weather, the women made vinegar water for the men to drink while they were working, and coffee with the meals.

Grandfather didn't like weeds, and for sure, he never did like seeing bunches of hay left on a field after it was harvested. He had a large scythe he used to cut down weeds and standing hay that had been missed. It needed sharpening every so often and I was included in the process of learning how to sharpen it. I would turn the handle on a very large emery wheel while Grandfather held the blade in place. The bottom of the wheel would be immersed with water that was contained in a tray below. With a cup, my job was to keep the tray full using a pail of water nearby.

Grandfather was often found in the field with his rake in the hot sun all day, raking up bunches of hay. I can still visualize him to this day, out in the field with his straw hat tight on his head. He was a hard worker and never left the field until the work was done for the day. (His straw hat remains one of my favorite mementoes of him.)

When harvest time came, my brother and I would shuck the small white navy beans and the red kidney beans. The plants were pulled out and piled in a small building called the "motor house" where our well pump was located. The beans were left in there to dry down for a week or so, and then when we'd come home from school, we'd take the beans out of each pod. Believe me, it was quite a long and tedious job!

In late fall, it was pig butchering time. Five to six pigs were butchered the first day and left to hang overnight. The next day was consisted of cutting up and grinding the meat. The farm women scraped the casings, which were then used for sausage making the following day.

It was such an exciting time to come home from school! Everyone was busy, with two people filling sausages, one person turning the stuffer, and another taking the sausages as they were completed. Yet another person was cooking the liver sausage as the meat sausage was being carried out to the smoke house. My brother and I would sneak into the smoke house after several days of sausage making. It smelled so good we'd have to sample it, taking a bite or two.

Another chore on the farm was feeding the cows grain, and it was all done with feed out of large burlap sacks. First, the oats were taken out of the granary, and at the time, I'd hold the sacks open while Grandfather shoveled them full. The bags were then put on the farm truck and taken to the feed mill in town to be ground up together with other ingredients—vitamins, minerals, and salt. When it was ready, it was loaded on the truck and put in the barn, ready for feeding.

As I became older, I helped Grandfather milk the cows, which I really enjoyed. There were two surge buckets that were used, held beneath a cow by a belt around her belly. The milk was emptied into a round strainer that was set on top of a milk can. The cans, when full, were placed on a cart and taken to the milk shed, which was located in the center of the yard. There, the cans were dropped into cold water in a holding tank to keep the milk cool until the milkman came to pick it up.

Very little was purchased for the farm at the grocery store. Meat, vegetables, milk, and eggs all came from the farm. Flour was purchased in 50-pound cotton sacks, along with other baking items such as baking powder, baking soda, chocolates, salt and sugar.

Forest Junction was a small town. It had two taverns, a shoe store, meat market, blacksmith shop, bank, and post office, as well as a couple of grocery stores, one being a General Merchandise Store which sold food, shoes, tools, and all sorts of things. Gold bond trading stamps, food rationing stamps for sugar, butter, and even gas, were common then. But shopping for the farm was very infrequent.

However, around Christmas time and occasionally throughout the year, we'd go shopping in big cities, such as Green Bay or Appleton, which were huge compared to the small town of Forest Junction that I grew up in. It was always exciting to ride up
on the escalator at the Woolworth Five and Dime Store in Green Bay!

During my elementary school years, most of my aunts and uncles got married and moved away, leaving just my brother, Aunt Norma, Grandfather, and I on the homestead.

It wasn't always *work* living on the farm. Behind the house was a pond, where, in winter, we had many good times ice skating. Then in summer, I'd catch polliwogs or tadpoles and put them in the cattle water tank up by the barn, or put them in small jars. In hot weather, we'd go swimming in the pond where Richard and I would have an afternoon of splashing fun.

Another fun experience not to be forgotten was Labor Day, when

Grandfather and I attended our county fair in Calumet County. Oh, how I always looked forward to going along with him! We'd pack a lunch and make a picnic out of it. Going on the rides was a very good time for me.

Such were many of the experiences of my growing up on the farm in the 1940s and 1950s. I learned to appreciate every day and the adventure it brought with it.

Marjorie May, Freshman School Photo, 1952

Bob

As my elementary years drew to a close, I graduated from eighth grade at Holmes School in May of 1952. Toward the end of that school year, I had entered a safety speech contest sponsored by the Brillion High School's Future Farmers of America chapter. Amazingly, my speech was selected by the judges as the first place winner. I was presented with a trophy before the entire high school student body as part of a meeting held in the high school gym. That presentation was made by the Future Farmers of America Chapter President, Bob Stanelle.

Bob was a senior in high school and an only child. He lived across the road from Grandfather's farm, and worked the family farm with his parents. After that presentation, he had set his eyes on me.

Little by little, we began to get more and more acquainted. There were times when we'd go roller skating together with the church youth group at Gem Roller Skating Rink in Appleton. At first, I was awkward on the rink, but I learned fast to enjoy the ease of the skates rolling beneath me.

Then there were the neighborhood birthday parties. When a husband or wife in the neighborhood had a birthday, neighbors would get together in the evening to play cards. The women played Canasta and the men would play Sheepshead. Each family would bring a cake, so there would be five to seven different cakes available to sample. Sandwiches, salads, and pickles made up a delicious lunch.

Robert, better known as Bob, or his nickname in high school—Lippy—would oft times come over with his parents. It was then he and I would spend time together. I enjoyed those moments, and looked forward to the next time. I'd also go across the road to Bob's folks' farm and help in the barn in little ways, just for the fact of being there with him.

With elementary school behind me now, it seemed like I was always sifting out things in my mind. What had all happened and what would happen now? The insecurities of life hadn't left me; what *would* the future hold? I'd think ahead to high school, going from a one-room school house to a huge school with many classrooms. Seeing the classrooms at the high school on Eighth Grade Day really intimidated me.

My brother, Richard, was a senior, so I wasn't alone when I entered the school my freshman year at thirteen years of age. Many times, Richard drove to school, so in place of taking the bus, I was happy to go along with him.

Before going to school in the morning, I continued to help Grandfather with chores and milking every day of the week. I was taught to drive our little "A" International tractor, to do field dragging and crushing, all in preparation toward crop planting. Uncle Bert did all the field work, so I was really helping him. Either way, I enjoyed doing it. Later, he purchased the farm from Grandfather.

In social activities, I was very active in 4-H. I also went regularly to Church Youth Fellowship meetings on Sunday evening. After the meetings, the older group would go out to a restaurant, and at times, to a late movie. I was happy to be invited along to go as part of the group. Bob was usually there, too.

Bob's folks owned a Lincoln Continental, a car of prestige at the time.

He'd be allowed to drive it occasionally, so when he'd pick me up, me being a freshman at the time and him being graduated from high school now, it was really cool for me. Little did I know what was to come!

In the subject of sex, everything was always "hush, hush" on the farm. My aunt never told me anything, and we didn't have classes in health about the human body in elementary school, either. I remember when my monthly menstrual cycles started. I was unaware of what was even happening; I was frightened, thinking something was definitely wrong with me. Later, in the second semester of freshman year, we learned about human anatomy, with a separate girls' class, as well as joint classes together with the freshman boys.

The girlfriends I had weren't really close friends to me. We never discussed or talked about anything, especially not sex. There wasn't anyone that I felt close to, that I would be confident to share secrets about myself. However, it wasn't very long after that my experiences taught me first-hand what I needed to know.

With hormones activated and a high school graduate showing his affection to me, I was a happy, soon-to-be sophomore. How great was that? I was elated, and felt like I was really somebody, until months later— only to find out that I was pregnant.

My brother, Richard, had gone off to join the US Marines after he graduated from high school in 1953. So it was Grandfather, Aunt Norma, and myself at home. As I started my second year of high school, I didn't tell anyone what had happened between Bob and me. But I was so confused and insecure. *What would I do now?*

The first person I told that I was pregnant was Bob, and it wasn't much after that his parents came to know the truth. I didn't know what to do; an abortion never entered my mind. Abortion wasn't as prevalent then as it is now. Unless someone had a miscarriage, most women would deliver a baby full-term no matter what the circumstances.

Bob's folks seemed to be sort of fond of me. It was their thoughts that prodded us to get married. We agreed with them, and Bob and I both knew in our hearts it was the right thing to do. It was evident we enjoyed spending time together.

Meanwhile, at the high school, I was chosen to be a "B" team cheerleader, which I was happy about, only to know reality wouldn't allow me to be one for very long. After about two months into the school year, my second year of high school ended. And I never returned.

Bob's folks made arrangements with a pastor at the Evangelical United Brethren Church in Dubuque, Iowa to conduct the marriage ceremony. We were unable to be married in Wisconsin because the legal age for marriage was sixteen, and I was only fourteen years old. The plans were set into motion for us to travel to Iowa on October 30, 1953.

The day came too soon, and we left for Dubuque. My brother came home on leave from the Marines to be a witness to the ceremony. He had just finished boot camp, and he was our best man. One of Bob's cousins, Barbara Covey, was my maid of honor. It was one full busy day!

I'll always remember the day after our wedding, though, when Bob and I went to visit Grandpa and Grandma Lingle, my dad's parents. I wore my wedding dress and Bob had on his suit. Being that it was October 31st, my grandparents thought we were dressing up for Halloween. They never expected to hear what we told them that day. I said, "Grandma, we were married yesterday." After the surprise wore off, they were very happy for us and wished us many great days together.

Thanksgiving Day on the Arthur Stanelle farm in Forest Junction, WI, 1954

Robert Jr.

The birth of our son on February 27, 1954 was difficult for me. I was not at ease at all, not knowing what to expect during childbirth. There weren't any Lamaze birthing classes back then, and I wasn't taught how to work with contractions. I didn't even know what a contraction was! I was so scared, and it was two and a half days of long hours in labor at the hospital before our son was born.

The baby had been positioned incorrectly, so it took two doctors to assist in the delivery of our nine pound, two and one-half ounce baby boy. I was told later that I nearly died. My hospital stay was almost two weeks. Needless to say, I was glad when it was all over.

Certainly now, life took on a whole new turn of events. With a new life to care for, I'd go to the baby's crib and watch him, wondering if he was still breathing. Perhaps as it is with most new moms, there was much anxiety, especially being a very young, new mother.

Soon after our son, Robert Jr., was born, Grandpa and Grandma Lingle became closer to me. I'd take him to visit them often, like on days when I had doctor appointments in Kaukauna, about a twenty-minute drive from home, so it always worked out to stop there afterwards. They were so happy to see me, and especially, their first great-grandchild.

Bob and I lived with his parents and had a large bedroom in the downstairs part of their house. Everything else was shared with his folks. His mom made the meals and even did all the laundry. Our marriage wasn't as a marriage should be—a man and a woman becoming one and leaving their parents, setting up a new home with a new family.

Robert Jr. was a healthy little boy. He was Bob's folks' pride and joy, and never lacked for attention, being the firstborn in our family and first grandchild. There were times I felt resentment towards Bob's mother; however, I wasn't unkind to her. She would take care of Robert Jr. while I'd work outside doing chores. More and more, I was pitching in to help on the farm. Sometimes I questioned myself, wondering if I was a hired girl or my husband's wife.

The farm consisted of approximately 375 acres of cropland, with a herd of over 100 head of Guernsey cows. It was a lot for a small family to take care of on a daily basis.

Planting time found me on the tractors again. One experience, which could have turned into a tragic one, happened while driving our big International "M" tractor, pulling chopper boxes full of forage from the field.

I was taking an empty chopper box out into the field, just leaving the farm yard, when Robert Jr., who was three years old, ran out after me, wanting to come along. Bob's mom came after him and wouldn't let him go with me on the tractor. It was a good thing, too.

On the way back from the field, going over a railroad track, the chopper box became loose, due to the hitch pin flying out of it. The box hit the tractor wheels while still moving, and the box crawled up, pinning me between the seat and the steering wheel. Had my son been in my lap that day, it could've been a fatal ride for him. I was badly bruised and sore, but thankfully had no broken bones. Still, it was quite a scare. I was so thankful Robert Jr. wasn't with me!

Our Growing Family

It wasn't too long after Robert Jr.'s first birthday that I realized I was pregnant again. Upon visiting the doctor, he confirmed it, and said I would have an autumn baby, about the second week in October. I was sixteen years old. There was so much excitement now, knowing that our son would be getting a sister or brother—but, not knowing which until after I gave birth, since there were no ultrasounds in those days. I looked forward to our second child, though rather reluctantly, because I'd had such a difficult labor and delivery with my first baby. I was worried I'd have the same trouble again.

The summer seemed to fly by rapidly. We, as a family, were active in 4-H. We showed our Guernsey cows at the local county fair. Getting the animals fitted and ready for show day made a lot of extra work, along with the daily farm chores and seasonal crop duties. Still, I enjoyed it.

Along with the coming of fall in 1955, the awaited day suddenly came with the birth of our second child. On October 15th, a baby girl, with lots of pitch black hair, weighing nine pounds, twelve ounces, was born.

Robert Jr. had been named after his great-grandfather, Robert Eick, and his great-grandfather, Arthur Stanelle, Sr., as well as his own dad. Our baby girl was named Kathryn Ann, after her two great-grandmothers, Kathryn Lingle and Anna Stanelle. But we called her Kathy. She was very easy to care for, good-natured, and not shy at all. Being my second child, I was much more at ease as her mother.

Having two children now, Bob's folks came up with the idea that the upstairs of the house could be remodeled into a separate apartment for us. A neighbor of ours, who was a carpenter, eagerly took on the job. It was several years before it was finished, but we knew it would be great to have our own separate space.

There were three bedrooms, plus one very small room used as the nursery. A living room, a large kitchen and one full bathroom made up our living quarters. Metal steps were installed on the side of the house for an outside entrance, but there were also steps inside for ease of interacting with my in-laws.

It was nice to have a kitchen for our own family. I now made meals, and through belonging to 4-H, our food and nutrition leader had taught us how to knead bread, bake sweet yeast rolls, cook vegetables properly, and make different meat cuts. To be ever working seemed to be my lot; there was always something needing to be done. Of course, that made time go by fast!

Another year had drawn to a close, and the start of 1957 was well on its way. We gave Robert Jr. his third birthday party in February on the 27th. It was small, only family there, but he enjoyed his cake just the same. Kathy would be two years old in the fall. They sure seemed to be growing up fast!

Grandma Stanelle (Bob's mom) would take care of the little ones while I worked out in the fields, in the barn, and when Bob and I would go to the 4-H meetings. It was convenient to have a built-in babysitter.

In the summer of 1957 came another surprise—another baby was on the way and due early in 1958. Bob and I were glad we lived upstairs now with more room, seeing that our family was increasing!

It was winter time, when on January 7th, 1958, Mary Ellen joined our family, weighing in at eight pounds, ten ounces. Although not as big as her older brother and sister, she was a healthy baby girl. We named her after her two great-grandmothers, Mary Eick and Ella Stanelle.

Mary Ellen had a special welcome, due to being the first baby born in our area in the New Year. A notice was put in the local newspaper, and many local businesses sent us gifts, which was an unexpected delight.

It seemed like the diapers and pins were never put away for very long. I was doing our own laundry, and back then, there weren't disposable diapers available for young mothers to use; just cloth diapers along with a diaper pail, where they'd soak before getting washed with a hand wringer wash machine and rinsed in two water tubs. It was hard work, but so worth it. A lot different than today's easy disposable diapers!

Nursing the babies was easy. When we'd milk the cows, the babies would sit comfortably in their infant seat, right on top of the milk bulk tank. The agitator, which stirred the milk, made a quiet humming sound, and the warm environment provided a perfect place for them out of harm's way.

Marjorie M. Beyersdorf
Thank You, Grandfather

Seeing that my move away from Grandfather's farm was just across the road, it made it very convenient for him to come and visit, or for me to stop by to see him. As he grew older, it was harder for him to shave himself. He'd always used a straight razor, and many times, he would cut himself due to his hurt shoulder and his unsteadiness.

He enjoyed coming over to see his great-grandchildren, too; usually about twice a week. We made arrangements according to my schedule; he'd come by and I would shave him with an electric shaver. It was hard for him to cut his fingernails and toenails, too, so I did that as needed to be done. There were days I'd go by to see him, too, when circumstances hindered him from coming over to our place.

Grandfather, being the dedicated farmer that he was and truly a man of the soil, had always said that when he died, he wanted it to be after all the harvesting and fall work was finished. He was granted his desire.

I received a phone call on December 9th, 1959, and was told that Grandfather had died. He was found lying on the kitchen floor. Being sick wasn't Grandfather's plight; he'd never been in the hospital, not on any prescriptions, and was always active for his eighty-eight years. I was asked if I wanted to go over to the house, but chose not to. Grandfather wasn't there anymore; he had gone on ahead!

It was because of living with Grandfather that I got my love of animals and the "way of life" on the farm. My thoughts go back to when I cared for Hilltop Anne, a registered pig my brother had. When Richard joined the US Marines, the pig was mine to take care of for the duration of his service. It was an exciting time when her little piglets were born, that's for sure.

I remember gathering eggs from the chickens, helping milk the cows, and feeding the baby calves. Then, there was all the garden work we did together. Coming into the house and seeing Grandfather sitting in his rocking chair, listening to the World News with Gabriel Heater, as he rested after a long day. These are my favorite memories of him I'll never forget. His chair still sits in my living room today.

Thank you, Grandfather, for who you were to me!

My Story: Faith, Family, Farm

Bob and Marjorie Stanelle Family Photo, Christmas 1964

Bob and Marjorie Stanelle Family Photo, 1969

Grandpa Stanelle

With 1959 drawing to a close, a new era approached; the 1960s. The "60s" as they were called, brought with it a lot of unrest in society, with riots on university and college campuses. President John F. Kennedy was shot and killed, which was quite a shock to our nation. It made me realize that we do live in a fallen world, and sin was running rampant.

The summer of 1962 was very hot. We were kept busy with getting the hay baled and elevated into the barn, stored away for winter's use. Following that was the harvesting of the grain.

Besides all the farm work, the 4-H Club continued to be a big part of our family's schedule. There were separate project meetings and monthly club meetings. Bob and I were both 4-H leaders, which meant assisting members with their projects, seeing that record books were being kept up, and helping out at the local county fair.

Calumet County Fair was always held over Labor Day weekend. Monday was Labor Day, and right after the holiday, Tuesday was the start-up of the school year. By now, Robert Jr. was entering fourth grade, Kathy was in third grade, and Mary Ellen would be starting her first day of kindergarten. It was a mixed emotional day for me.

After the children were off to school, there was all that was brought home from the county fair to still deal with. Cleaning out the show box (used for cattle showing) with so much to be put away and a lot of dirty clothes to wash—a real work-packed day.

Remodeling had been planned and started within the barn. The old cow stanchions were replaced with new comfort stalls. Each cow now could lay down with her neck by her side and have more "moving around" space. Summer had been very, very busy! Not only with getting the crops planted and getting hay cut and brought in, but the remodeling and cementing was ongoing, too. If I thought the days were going fast before, they were really breezing by now!

Finally, we bought an automatic barn cleaner. It was great! Before, the gutters behind the cows were cleaned out with a shovel by hand. Manure was put into a wheelbarrow and wheeled onto a large wooden plank that was set up vertically into the manure spreader. Having the automatic barn cleaner would make things a lot easier.

Weeks of a lot of extra work went by, and now fall was presenting its own routine work with the corn silage that needed to be harvested. Next, it was the preparation for winter, with cutting wood and hauling it into the basement for our wood furnace. Before long, Thanksgiving Day would be here, and we eagerly looked forward to my mother-in-law's delicious dinner of turkey and potato dumplings!

Outside, the leaves were changing into their own beautiful colors, signifying autumn was here. It was at this time that my father-in-law (Bob's dad) was making arrangements to have surgery on a hernia, which he had for a long time. Little did we know on that cold day in mid-November of 1962, as he entered the hospital, that he'd never come home again.

We soon learned that the doctors had made a discovery in the beginning process of the surgery. He was full of cancer in his liver and pancreas. We made many trips to the hospital in Appleton. My mother-in-law and Aunt Ede (his sister) took turns staying with him.

Because Bob's dad was absent from the farm, work intensified for Bob and I. It wasn't easy with the visits to the hospital, and keeping up with all the work. At one point, I recall Grandpa Lingle coming to the farm and staying overnight for several days to help out with chores.

Christmas time was different this year, with Grandpa Stanelle in the hospital. We visited him as often as we could. On a shopping trip, Robert Jr. had received a new pair of shoes, and he wanted to show them to Grandpa. So, before running home, we went to the hospital for a quick visit. Upon seeing the shoes, Grandpa Stanelle said, "Wow, you are growing up! Your shoes are almost as big as Grandpa's already!" Yes, Robert Jr. was growing up; eight years old and already a big help on the farm.

The winter was really cold, with many days with below freezing temperatures, but the time seemed to go by fast. Spring was soon knocking on the door of time, and with it came the day of my father-in-law's death. I had taken my mother-in-law to the hospital; Aunt Ede was staying with him at the time. We were all in the room together when he took his last breath. After a long hospital stay of five months, at the age of sixty-two, my father-in-law had died. The day was April 30th, 1963.

The funeral arrangements were made, and we'd need to be there for my mother-in-law. Many people came to offer sympathy and help, and also brought food to the house. With my father-in-law gone, we were now farming on our own. A lot of new challenges lie ahead for Bob and me.

New Life!

What was life all about? Things never really seemed to add up. This was a time where life for me was just easier to opt out of, or so I thought. Being thrust into an early marriage, becoming a very young mother so soon after, when all I could do was work, work, work...I can't say I didn't enjoy working; however, there seemed to be no meaning or purpose to life. Everything was so "daily"!

It was June 23, 1963 when, as a very distraught, uneasy, and depressed person, I called my pastor. The day was hot and sticky, and we were baling hay. After lunch, the pastor came to our home. I literally erupted emotionally! I shared my hurts, my emptiness, and how life to me seemed so meaningless, even though I lacked nothing in a material or physical way.

The pastor prayed with me and spoke of how in the Scriptures, the *Holy Bible*, we are told that we not only have a body and mind; there is also a spiritual part of us. God created us as a living soul. He created us to have fellowship with Him. However, from the beginning, disobedience resulting in sin has passed on to every person. He read from God's Word. "All have sinned and come short of the glory of God" (Romans 3:23).

Sin broke fellowship with God, who is perfect and holy, and cannot look upon sin. God in the Person of His Son, Jesus, came into the world, born of a virgin. He came to die and shed His Blood to pay the penalty of sin. "By His own blood, He entered once into the holy places, having obtained eternal redemption for us" (Hebrews 9:12b). Crucified, dead, and buried, He arose! Victorious over sin and death!

As the pastor talked, suddenly it gripped me. I had memorized many Bible verses in Sunday school; I had gone to catechism and was confirmed.

These were all the right things to do. Now, I realized it was mental activity—that it was only the outer surface. In my heart, I knew I needed Jesus to be my very own personal Savior.

I wept, and with repentance in my heart, prayed to God asking for His forgiveness. I received the Gift of Salvation through faith in God and His Word. "For the wages of sin is death, but the gift of God is eternal life through Jesus Christ our Lord" (Romans 6:23).

Ever since that day, June 23, 1963, life was different for me. It was like a weight had been lifted. It wasn't different in the work schedule, housework, caring for the children, farm work, and the like. There was that Special Person, Jesus my personal Savior, who I could go to. I could pray to God. Jesus was the mediator. "There is one God, and one Mediator between God and men, the man Christ Jesus" (1 Timothy 2:5). The Bible was no longer a stranger to me. I would read it, searching and studying it every chance I'd get.

December of 1963 was my first Christmas that I really knew it wasn't all about gifts, except for "The Gift" —God's Son, Jesus, who came to be the Savior of the world. I was so thankful that Jesus was my own personal Savior now, a reality in my life! During those months especially, I needed God's words and His comfort, and even more so, I'd need them in the months ahead.

Christmas 1963 was an exciting time for our children, with their school and church Christmas programs happening. At church, there was a Christmas Eve service that the children all took part in. After the evening milking and chores (which always seemed to get finished quickly that day), we got ready to go to the Christmas Eve program. After it was finished, bags of candy and fruit were handed out to each child.

Upon arriving home, there was excitement as the children found lots of presents under our Christmas tree. My brother, his wife and son, Mike, were with us, and sometimes an aunt and uncle came by, too. A good time was had by all in the opening up of our gifts, all because of the Greatest Gift given, Jesus our Savior!

The late evening ended with Christmas cookies, stolen, salads, sandwiches, and punch.

My Story: Faith, Family, Farm

Farming as a Family

The '60s were really "gung ho," meaning it was an extremely enthusiastic time on the farm. In the spring of 1964, we bought a 20' x 60' Harvestor with an automatic bunk and auger for year-round feeding. This allowed the cows to be fed outside with no handwork involved. Then later, in the fall of that same year, we built a 50' x 90' pole barn for young stock and machinery storage space.

Not only were there new building additions happening on the farm, but a new addition would be joining our family in the fall. I was so thankful this pregnancy seemed to agree with me. There was minimal discomfort. In fact, I worked outside in the barn right up to the day I went to the hospital.

The delivery itself wasn't so easy though, mostly because I didn't work with my contractions. I made it through, and on September 29th, 1964, a bouncing baby boy was born, weighing eight pounds, twelve ounces. We named him Richard John, after his only uncle, Richard (my brother), and his paternal grandfather, John (my dad).

Not only did aunts and uncles come to our home to see our new son, but even 4-H Club members came, bringing gifts for the baby. Now, our family was made up of two boys and two girls, and the cloth diapers were back in use. Our other children really liked their baby brother. For sure, the girls always wanted to hold him.

As 1964 ended, with all its new additions, the new additions still didn't end! Yes, more building. This time a 20' x 27' high-moisture corn unit was built as a Harvestore was added. Plus, at the end of the year, a calf barn was remodeled. One of our neighbors made the comment, "On the farm, when you start building, you'll never quit." How true it was with our farm!

Along came 1966, and we were still building. This time, it was an 18' x 21' new milk house that we constructed. Inside the building would be a new milk bulk tank, along with a permanent dumping station. The old milk house was very small. Having more space, with an office and indoor bathroom adjacent to the new milk house was so convenient. Plus, we had added to the farm a new feature, in that it was switched over to three-phase electric current, thereby reducing our electricity costs.

We did "farming" as a family. Robert Jr. was twelve years old; Kathy was eleven and Mary Ellen eight, with little Richard John being our two-year-old tagging along. The children each had their chores. There were also their 4-H calf projects, along with other projects like rabbits, chickens, cooking, and grains, all to be taken for judging at the county fair.

Marjorie M. Beyersdorf

Time continued to march along, and when Robert Jr. was in his junior and senior years of high school, he worked after school at a local cheese factory. He wasn't exactly a "farmer at heart."

The girls were excellent workers in the barn, helping milk the cows, cleaning out calf pens by hand, and feeding the calves. It was nice to work together with them. I milked the cows with Bob each morning and night. Keeping the milk house clean, keeping all the farm records, field work when in season, housework, and caring for the family was a lot to do. Outside of all of this were the 4-H responsibilities, plus teaching a Sunday school class as well. There never seemed to be a time when I'd have a situation where I could say, "There is nothing to do!"

The turn of events in the '60s was soon to be history in the annals of time, with the completion of all the remodeling and the newly built facilities, and the joys of having our second son, Richard John, joining the family. It was a joyous time for me. I enjoyed living in the country, especially being on the farm, because of my love of animals and working out-of-doors in the serenity of nature.

Marjorie and Bob Stanelle Family Photo, Easter, 1969-Kathy made the dresses

Marjorie, Kathy, and Bob Stanelle at the National Guernsey Pageant, 1973

The '70s

With a flip of the calendar, the '70s were here! The years passed by faster and faster, and the children were growing up quickly. Richard John ("Richie") would be entering school. As I accompanied him to get on the school bus on his first day, there was a big lump in my throat knowing our little boy was now entering the "big world" by himself. All the children were in school now and there was an excitement of sharing about the activities of the day when they arrived home in the afternoon.

Progress in Agriculture was recognized by the Brillion Jaycees, and Bob and I were chosen as the "Outstanding Young Farmer" to represent our Jaycees Chapter in the local area and at the State level, along with other OYF farmers. We were treated to a large banquet given by the Jaycees, and awarded a plaque with our names engraved on it. Along with all that, we received publicity, including pictures of us in the local newspaper.

Having an all-Guernsey herd on our farm, our family was active in the Guernsey activities, locally and at the state level. On Valentine's Day of 1972, our daughter, Kathy was in the competition for the State Guernsey Princess. We were happy along with her, when at the evening's grand banquet, she was crowned the 1972-73 State Guernsey Princess. This made her eligible to be entered into the National Guernsey Queen competition, which would be held in Orlando, Florida in April of 1973. (Our family later received an all-expense paid trip to the convention, which was quite the event.)

Graduation time was drawing near, and Robert Jr. was a member of the class of 1972. Going to watch him play football on the school "A" team for the Brillion Lions was now a thing of the past. No more attending the band concerts, either, where he participated as a drummer. With a large gathering of people: aunts, uncles, friends, and classmates, we celebrated his graduation.

During his last year of high school, Robert Jr. had apprenticed as an electrician at the Brillion Iron Works. Now with high school graduation completed several months ago, along came a big event! On October 7th, 1972, Robert Jr. married our pastor's daughter, whom he'd been dating for quite a while.

Bob and I helped them get a new trailer home, set it up on a tract of land on our farm out near a woodlot, right off of Highway 57. Robert Jr. was a very determined young man. He worked hard in whatever he wanted to achieve.

For me, life was unfolding ever so swiftly, not all of it pre-planned.

Happy Joe's birthday event for Richard, 1972

My Story: Faith, Family, Farm
Too Much!

In the early fall of 1972, I had gone to the doctor for what I knew would be his answer—I was pregnant. With the workload on the farm and being involved in outside responsibilities—I was a 4-H Club main leader, project leader, Sunday school teacher and the Sunday school superintendent—how would I handle all this, plus a pregnancy? It was hard for me to accept it because each of my other deliveries had been so very hard.

I'll never forget the time when I took a little purple car that we had and just drove, with no destination in mind, wanting to get away from it all! As I drove, the view along the roadside was beautiful. The trees were in an array of many colors, showing off their fall beauty.

As the sun was getting ready to set below the horizon, I spotted a lane in a farmer's field. Thinking no one would bother me there, I drove down the lane and it took me to the edge of a large woodlot far off the main road. I had taken my Bible with me, and that night I read till it was too dark to see. I cried and prayed, and prayed and cried. "God, help me to go on!"

Thankfully, there was a blanket in the car and it came in handy, because that night was very cold. It was hard to lie down, being as I was in such a compact vehicle, but I was so tired. I fell asleep, and I awoke to a very bright sunrise. It was beautiful.

"Now what do I do?" I asked aloud to the empty car. I knew I'd have to go back home eventually; however, I drove first to our pastor's home in Appleton. Not having eaten much the day before and being emotionally in a quandary, the pastor's wife saw my plight.

She said, "You look quite pale, Marjorie," and made me some tea and toast to eat. Sharing with them that I was pregnant again was difficult for me, especially not knowing how I'd go on. My pastor told me that he'd talk to Bob and suggest that we cut back on the farm work.

I arrived back home knowing I couldn't quit. So with a change of mind and attitude, I took hold of all the responsibilities again.

Marjorie M. Beyersdorf
Daughters

The winds of autumn were briskly blowing the tree leaves in all their previous splendor. They'd lie on the ground, ready for winter's entry. The season's change meant getting prepared for what came next. Firewood needed to be hauled in, split, and thrown down into the basement for storing. All the while in doing so, I was looking forward to a cozy, warm house and enjoying the times of eating popcorn while watching a good television program.

On occasion, we'd make homemade ice cream, a great winter treat for the kids. Chunks of ice were gathered from our pond and put into a gunny sack. Then we'd pound the sack upon the ground to break the ice inside into small particles. The ice was put around the inner sides of the wooden ice cream maker, with the metal gallon container in the center. The container was then filled with a mixture of rich Guernsey cream, sugar, and vanilla. This was churned with a handle until it was thickened. Oh, how delicious it was!

Christmas time brought with it a tradition between our neighbors. We'd visit each other's homes and show the gifts our families received for Christmas. It was a fun time of relaxing, visiting, and eating Christmas goodies. Usually, we would make homemade ice cream when the neighbors came to visit, too.

The calendar on the wall changed to 1973. The first few months passed by fast, with all the activities and work. My doctor had said the baby should arrive mid-March and he was right. I went into the hospital on March 14, with the delivery not happening until the following evening. Other gals came into the labor room and went out, and I was still there!

Lanetta May was born at 7:30 PM on March 15th, 1973 weighing nine pounds, seven ounces. The Guernsey Queen before our daughter Kathy was crowned was called Lynette, which was a name Bob and I liked. We changed it somewhat by inserting an "a" for the "y" and an "a" on the end in place of the "e", spelling it Lanetta. May is my middle name, and now it would be the baby's middle name, too.

I hardly got home from the hospital, and adjusted to our precious little newcomer, before we as a family found ourselves preparing for a trip to Florida. I had a slight infection, prompting my doctor to send antibiotics along with me. We drove the long distance from Wisconsin to Florida in our Lincoln Continental car. Among the baby gifts we received was a little yellow canvas papoose carrier. The straps could be adjusted over my shoulders, and little Lanetta was kept close on my chest. It was great to have, especially with all the walking I did. Robert Jr. took care of the chores and milking while we were gone, but thankfully he did have extra help. Our departure date was March 30th and we returned home on April 9th.

Kathy reigned throughout the year, attending other state Guernsey conventions in Iowa, California, and Illinois, to name a few. She was kept busy all year. The sightseeing and tours had been enjoyable, but most important of all was that Kathy was crowned the 1973-74 National Guernsey Queen!

Kathy graduated from high school with the high honor of being the valedictorian of her class of 1973. That September 4th, she began her college career at Olivet Nazarene College in Kankakee, Illinois, studying to be a registered nurse. We had so many blessings in our lives.

Hired Help

With Kathy's hands absent now from doing barn chores, the workload certainly wasn't any lighter. I had approached Bob with several solutions, from cutting back on cows (which expenses would hardly allow), to getting hired help, to the extreme of him finding a different wife. The work demands were high.

The decision was made to put an advertisement in the paper for "Help Wanted" on the farm. It wasn't long before a fellow came down our lane in an old truck. He had been honorably discharged not very long ago from the US Army. His dad had died when he was twelve years old and his mom had recently remarried. He knew he wouldn't want to live at home, so when he saw our ad, it caught his eye and he called. So, we said, "Yes, he's hired."

As our family grew, Robert Jr. had moved downstairs into Grandma's larger bedroom. Grandma agreed to let Milan Beyersdorf stay in the vacant bedroom that had been Robert Jr's. It was located right below the inside stairway.

Milan chimed right in with the work, which made our load lighter. To have help in cleaning out pens and operating the bunk to feed the cows was much appreciated. He was handy in fixing things like broken gates, and cow chains, and making fence repairs in the cow yard.

Bob was involved in a lot of outside activities. He was a volunteer fireman, with meetings once a week. He played dart ball with the church team, was a local school board member, and attended Forest Junction Civic League meetings, as well as the town board meetings. But now, the kids and I weren't finishing the work alone when Bob would have to go, at times, leaving early for a meeting. Milan helped wrap up the evening chores. Work wasn't such drudgery now. I'd help Milan and he would help me. I did his laundry and baked extra goodies when it could be squeezed in between the routine farm work.

We allowed Milan to take off some weekends so he could go see his brothers in Appleton. It felt empty on the farm when he was gone. We worked together very well. In fact, too good I suppose, as I reached out with a need, wanting to be cared for, and I sensed his similar need. We got to know each other in the following weeks, and before long, we were not only friendly with each other, but attracted to one another.

Yes, another unexpected action in my life! I was pregnant, but not with my husband's child. In my heart, I knew this for a fact, because Bob and I weren't intimate with each other. *How could I ever live with this? How could I go on?*

But I did. For a while I lived on, concealing the truth, not knowing what would happen next. I continued to carry on with each day's work, with the family household work, and in the barn. In the fall of 1974, I had a doctor's appointment and he confirmed the pregnancy. The next baby to be born would be in mid-April. I continued on, day to day with many mixed emotions. It wasn't easy to live a lie! No one would even suspect the real truth.

Gone

Winter was now here, with its brisk winds, cold air and a lot of snow. It seemed to be so drawn out, a very long winter! The weeks passed slowly. Toward the end of the year, Milan found a different job. He moved out and stayed with his sister in Milwaukee. He got work with her husband at a meat packing plant there.

I looked forward to spring, which was still aways off yet, although days usually moved fast on the farm. Like a flash, March appeared on the calendar. Lanetta would soon be celebrating her second birthday on the 15th. No diapers anymore; she was easy to potty train. Only now, I had more diapers to look forward to, but at least disposable diapers were available!

My Story: Faith, Family, Farm

Ironically, Robert Jr. and his wife were expecting their first child. Evan James Stanelle was born on February 7, 1975, our first grandchild. As a grandmother at age 36, my sixth baby would be due soon.

Oftentimes, I'd think of myself as a misfit. Married so young, I didn't fit in with my own age group anymore, and I was much too young to be comfortable with older couples. Still feeling somewhat ill-at-ease, the time was fast approaching for my baby to arrive. The robins had come back, the tulips were blooming, and it was an enjoyable time of the spring season.

I had a nine pound, eight ounce baby boy on April 23, 1975, to whom we gave the name Jeffrey (after my doctor) with a middle name Joseph, after his paternal great grandfather. It was very hard to conceal the truth I knew in my heart that no one else knew. Milan knew, but he was no longer working at the farm. He left before Jeffrey was born. It wasn't an easy time for me; I had failed God and my family.

With all the work needing to be done, a two-year-old underfoot, and a new baby, things never got easier. In my heart, there was too much guilt and hurt. It was getting harder and harder to go on. Not being plagued with headaches, but with heartaches, after one year, I had to get away!

On March 19th, 1976, I packed as much as I could of the two younger children's clothes and my own personal belongings into a second car we had, an older Chevy Impala, and I left the farm with Lanetta and Jeffrey.

At the time, Mary was a senior in high school and Richie was in sixth grade. It hurt so much to leave them, especially with Richie, him being so much younger. Before I left, I had gone out into the barn, and with tears in my eyes, I shared my good-byes with the cows, knowing there would be no more going out by them again.

Looking back now, I never thought of what my family would go through. Bob, Mary, Richie, and my mother-in-law still lived on the farm. Kathy, of course, was in college at the time. They didn't know where we went; they only knew we were gone.

Prior to leaving, I had gone to see an attorney, and he had suggested I move away for several weeks and stay with friends or relatives. Getting away from the present circumstances could give a person a new perspective, he had told me. Thus, I had moved away from the farm, with only more complications ahead.

I found a house for rent, located on the east side of Appleton. It was ready to be moved into. Not even having to put any money down, I was able to just move in! The owner was very kind. After I was all settled in, I paid the first month's rent with a little savings I had.

Weeks went by before Bob knew where I lived. After he found out where we were, he and Richie would come to visit quite often in the evenings, encouraging me to come back to the farm. On one of his visits, Bob brought me a dozen roses. But I couldn't go back. I wished it would've all been a dream and I'd wake up, not having to face all that I was!

I had contacted Milan and he knew that we weren't living on the farm anymore. He came to visit some weekends to see Jeffrey.

What the rest of my family didn't know was that I was pregnant again with my seventh child. Needless to say, my emotions would be like an ocean tide many times, riding high on the wave lengths!

One Hundred Percent Mom

The spring of 1976 was Mary's graduation year. Similar to the prior two graduation parties for Robert and Kathy, friends and relatives came to the house for a time of congratulations and visiting, along with good food and a delicious graduation cake. The party was held at the farm, and for a day, it felt like old times.

It was our country's centennial year, but it was also a severe drought year. Folks didn't have to cut their lawns; the grass was so dry it wouldn't grow. The temperatures were extremely high; dry and hot!

Certainly, it was a whole new life for me. This year, there'd be no working in the barn. The children had one hundred percent of their mom's time, so a couple times a week we would go to a park a few blocks away from our house. It had a large swimming pool and a kiddy pool, which we took advantage of in the hot summer.

On July 20th, while en route to a doctor's appointment, my car was struck on the driver's right rear side by another car that ran a stop sign. Upon seeing the oncoming car, I stepped on the accelerator to avoid the hit. But by doing so, and with the impact of the collision, my car flew fifty-seven feet over an embankment and landed upright in a resident's garden.

Being pregnant at the time, the police were concerned about me and an ambulance was called as a precaution, taking us to Kaukauna Community Hospital. Jeffrey had a bad cut by his lip, but Lanetta and I had no injuries, except a few bruises.

Being pregnant in excessive heat was very uncomfortable, especially so in the last weeks before the baby was born. The hot summer continued on right up to September 8th, which was the day of the delivery for my baby, who I named Jeremy Jon. Jeremy was a popular name at the time, so it was the name I chose. He was a big baby boy, weighing in at ten pounds, eleven ounces.

I needed minor surgery after the childbirth, and spent a total of twelve days in the hospital. Jeffrey and Lanetta were cared for at the home of Jim and Wanda, some of my friends from church.

While I was hospitalized, Grandma Lingle died, and I wasn't able to go to the wake or the church service. I hadn't seen her in quite some time and I felt bad about that. Grandma will always be remembered for all her kindness to me. Never did I leave their home empty-handed. She always sent something along with me home, be it food, fruit, a kettle, a scarf, or whatever she had for me that day. Going to Grandpa and Grandma's house had been like my second home.

When I was discharged from the hospital, I was so happy to have my brother bring me and my new son, Jeremy Jon, home. Being all so very awkward, not living on the farm anymore, still being married to Bob yet not having his child, it was great to have my brother back for a visit from his home in Arizona.

As the fall winds began to blow, it was so refreshing. They brought a welcome relief from an unusually hot summer. Mary was furthering her education by attending Lake Shore Technical Institute in Cleveland, Wisconsin, located near Manitowoc.

Caring for the younger children was my main priority now. Lanetta liked to hold the baby. She was three-and-a-half years old, with Jeff just about one-and-a-half. They kept me occupied.

It was a good thing, too, since I had dropped out of church activities and attendance. There wasn't any more 4-H involvement and no farm work for me, either. I stopped doing everything dead cold when I had left the farm. It was quite a time of transition for me.

I knew Christmas time would be different this year. We had a small Christmas tree in our rented home that the kids decorated. Many times, we'd go to the Goodwill store and find unique things for gifts. I remember one evening when the youth from the church came to our place singing Christmas carols. Among the group was my daughter, Kathy. She had taken a leave from college, and besides that, it was Christmas vacation for her anyway.

We visited the farm and were together on Christmas day, but it would never be the same. In my life, there was such unsettledness about it all. Here I was, living as a single mom with my three children, having launched out on my own!

Marjorie M. Beyersdorf
Kathy

The beginning of 1977 found us moving from our rented house into a townhouse not far off Highway 41, south of the city of Neenah. This was for easier access, being closer to Milwaukee. Milan would visit periodically, and we also drove to his apartment. There was no commitment from Milan to me; however, I knew he loved his boys and me.

Moving again put us closer to a Laundromat. We didn't have a washer or dryer at either place. Once a week, sometimes more, I took the dirty clothes and loaded them into the car, and off we'd go. The kids enjoyed the adventure and it took us out of our townhouse for a little while.

While in our townhouse, Kathy came over, and we had a nice visit together. She was now working as a Surgical Technician at the Kaukauna Community Hospital. She brought with her a pair of dress slacks, which needed to be shortened, and asked me to do it for her.

It was the last weekend of February when the children and I drove to visit Milan in Milwaukee. That Sunday afternoon, I received a phone call from a police officer telling me I was needed at home. Kathy Stanelle had *expired*. He didn't say she was killed, or died, nor dead, but just stated that *she had expired*. Those words didn't seem to sink into my mind.

It was February 27, 1977—Robert Jr.'s birthday. I learned quickly what happened. Kathy was driving home to the farm, and about two miles from it, she was struck broadside by a big pick-up truck and thrown from her vehicle. She was pronounced dead at Theda Clark Hospital in Neenah several hours later.

I wasn't really in fellowship with God as I had been in the past. Prayer had become a stranger, even though I knew God was not. Yet, as I was driving to the farm that day, I turned on the car radio to the Christian station and every song that played was a song of comfort. God is faithful; He knows all. How timely!

When I arrived at the farm, I was told that Kathy had worked the morning shift at the hospital. She was coming home to the farm for Robert Jr.'s birthday. Her brother was going to take them out for dinner. Instead, upon notification of the accident, Robert Jr. drove to Theda Clark and saw Kathy at the hospital, where she was unconscious. She didn't have any cuts or abrasions on her; a massive head injury was the cause of her death.

It was certainly a shock to everyone! One of my cousins made the statement, "This is so unfair! A talented young person, twenty-one years of age, with so much life ahead of her…" Since that time, I've come to realize that God is no respecter of persons. He takes young and old; He holds the key to death (Revelation 1:18).

The church was full of people for Kathy's service, even state and national representatives were there, with her association as the recently passed State Guernsey Princess and National Guernsey Queen.

I didn't shed a lot of tears that week. I was beyond shock. However, a couple of months later, I drove out to the cemetery and bawled like a baby. Afterwards, I went to Grandfather's farm (which was now my uncle's farm) to see Aunt Norma, who lived there still, and on the davenport, I cried some more. We talked about past times together with Kathy and how loved she was; how the previous fall, Kathy, the children, and I had picked apples together in an apple orchard in Little Chute. I told Aunt Norma my last words with Kathy were about something trivial, when she had brought her slacks over for me to hem. I never knew that would be the last time I'd see her alive.

I'm so thankful that Kathy knew Jesus! She made the choice to give her life over to Him when she accepted and claimed Him to be her Savior and Lord. At age ten, on April 14, 1966, in her own words in her autobiography, she stated, "I received Christ as my Savior. I want my life to tell for Him. This was the most important decision I made in my life." Her bold expressions in public about Jesus certainly touched many lives. We *will* be together again!

New Home

During that summer, there were mediation meetings regarding the custody of our daughter, Lanetta. Knowing now that I had divorce proceedings initiated, Bob wanted custody of her. It was finally agreed upon that she would stay with Bob, seeing Grandma and Mary were there to help care for her. I know it wasn't an easy time for her, nor was it for me. One of her frequent comments was, "I wish I could be cut in half—half with Mommy and half with Daddy!" We always stayed in touch and I'd go out to visit the farm. The apron strings were cut, but never the heart strings!

My divorce was finalized on September 17, 1977. Walking up to the Outagamie County Court House, the leaves were swirling around on the sidewalk, having just fallen from the trees. It was a season of life in nature that had ended for them. So it was for me; a marriage of twenty-four years and thirteen days was ended by man. The judge announced the divorce as final. Leaving so much behind me, not knowing what lay ahead of me, I took it all one day at a time.

During one of Milan's visits with the boys and I, he said, "I've purchased a newly built house in Saukville, a small city south of Milwaukee." He had a buddy of his living with him at the time. But as time went on, instead of him driving every weekend to see us, he wanted us to move, and live with him. I finally agreed, and we moved to Saukville in the latter part of '77.

Milan and I met several friends who were attending a Baptist church in Saukville, and we started attending church there together as a family. Milan had a brother who lived in Saukville, too, which made it easier to settle in.

Our new home was a three-bedroom house located way down on a dead end street. The lot was large enough for a garden, so we planted veggies and tomatoes. Milan had gotten a large German Shepherd named King, and there was plenty of area for him to run, too. There was also a large hill just west of us. In the winter, Bob brought Lanetta for a visit and she and the boys had a good time sliding down the big hill.

Another Christmas time came, and this one was surely different again as we went out to the farm on Christmas Eve to be together with my family. How well I remember the drive back to Saukville in the wee hours of the morning. We slept right away upon arriving home, and the boys opened their presents when we awoke. It was Christmas day, and their excitement was contagious!

Each morning, I could now see Milan off to work as he went to the meat packing plant in Milwaukee. I'd make his lunch, and in doing so, my thoughts would often be of my mother as she was preparing lunch for Dad.

Here we were; Milan and I living together and not married. We believed the right thing to do was to have a marriage ceremony in the church. Our friends, Harry and Virginia, heartily agreed; and in fact, they wanted to be our witnesses. The date was set for May 13, 1978.

Our wedding was held at River Bend Baptist Church in Saukville. Lanetta was with us for a stay while the rest of the family was gone to a state Guernsey convention for the weekend. It worked out well, and Lanetta was our flower girl, with Jeff being the ring bearer. Aunt Norma, Uncle Harry, and Aunt Verna were present, along with Milan's mom, stepdad, brothers and sisters. Our friend, Virginia had a cake business in her home and she made our wedding cake for us. The church folks prepared a wedding meal. It was a lovely day!

Discipline

When I had lived in Neenah in the townhouse, there was an elderly man, Matt, who knew my paternal grandparents. I often picked him up and took him grocery shopping, as he didn't drive. One time, we went out to the Memorial Cemetery in Appleton to look up my dad's gravesite.

Matt had his living quarters above a tavern in Kaukauna. It had several bedrooms, which he rented out to Kaukauna paper mill workers. Now that he was getting older, he wanted to end the rentals. Not having ever been married, and with no remaining relatives, he gave me all his furniture and belongings. I had left most of my belongings behind on the farm, taking only the basics of what I needed. And now, I had so much! There were many antique dressers, a writing desk, china cabinet, kitchen table and chairs, and a lot of books, of which all came to the house in Saukville. I recall that we also had a rummage sale for Matt in the basement of the townhouse to sell the remaining items.

I took on the project of refinishing the furniture. Being very old, it was dark varnish, so I sanded away and did a lot of staining. As I was restoring the furniture to a new finish, my thoughts were of how God would have to refinish and restore me.

Yes, the sanding of God's discipline hurts! It's God's way of allowing us to go our own way. In the Bible, Isaiah 53:6 tells us, "We all like sheep have gone astray. We have turned, every one to his own way; and the LORD hath laid on him the iniquity of us all." God forces no one to come to Him, to love Him, nor to obey His Word. However, He did make a way for us to come to Him and to know Him, through His Incarnate Son, Jesus, upon Whom He laid the sins of us all.

I had accepted Jesus as my personal Savior back in 1963. As I looked back to that day, there was a lot of studying and me doing the Lord's work in the church. But, we can be so busy doing the "work of the Lord" that we sometimes forget the "Lord of the work" —*not in close fellowship with Him at all.*

Marjorie M. Beyersdorf

Marjorie with Jeffrey and Jeremy, 1978

Moving Again!

A couple months had passed. It was a Sunday in July after church, when upon finishing our noon meal, Milan was reading the *State Agri-View*. He came across a For Sale ad—a farm in Wausau, including cows, machinery, and buildings. It was ready to purchase and be taken over.

Milan had a desire to have his own farm someday. His dad's farm was east of Wausau, where Milan grew up until his dad's death, when Milan was twelve years old. So, the area wasn't unfamiliar to him. "Let's drive up and check it out," he said.

I could tell how eager he was to see the property. Although it wasn't preplanned, we were on our way, on a three-and-a-half hours' drive, heading north to Wausau.

Upon seeing it all, Milan was excited. That following week, we contacted

My Story: Faith, Family, Farm

Farmers' Home Administration to see about getting a loan. They handed us application forms to fill out, and set up a return appointment. We put a For Sale sign up in front of our house, not even knowing if the farm deal would work out.

Questions loomed in my mind. Just two years and four months ago, I had left my husband, family, and the farm. A year and a half later I was divorced, and in the eight months' time that had passed, was remarried. Now, a couple of months after our wedding, we were looking to purchase a farm. Life certainly was occurring "in the fast lane!"

After several contacts with the Farmers' Home Administration, our loan applications were approved. Our hope now was to sell the house—and quickly! My friend, Virginia and I put our hands on the FOR SALE sign, making our request to God in prayer.

In October, an offer was made on the house, and later was signed. There was a financial gain in the sale, all of which was to be applied toward our farm purchase. By December 19th, 1978, we had to be out of our Saukville house, but the loan wouldn't be available till year end.

Thankfully, the farm owners were very kind! They allowed us to move all our furniture and things down into their basement, which was a very large area. This was considerate of them; we didn't need to look for a storage place. For a week, we lived with friends—the couple who were our wedding attendants. It was amazing to see how things had worked out!

We moved into the farm house right after Christmas. However, the farm family of eight children and their parents, whom we had bought the property from, hadn't moved anything out until December 29th. The house had six bedrooms, and we slept upstairs. Having the family there yet was good. They showed us their operation as we milked the cows together. It sure was better than taking over the farm stark cold!

It was a different Christmas observance this time. It was a transition time, which seemed to be my lot. The sixth time of change! And on December 29th, 1978 (Milan's birthday), the purchase papers were signed and we became owners of a 171-acre farm located northeast of Wausau, in the township of Texas. We began with 39 cows, young stock, and machinery.

Several days later, as we were looking out the living room window and seeing across the road all the fields and the woods, my husband said, "It's all ours now!"

I started crying; all my mixed emotions overwhelming me. For over twenty-three years, I had partnered in farming. I had known the challenges, endurance, and the ups and downs of it all. Milan had never farmed on his own. God alone knew what was ahead of us.

Marjorie M. Beyersdorf

Double M Faith Farm, 1980s

Farm Life...Again!

It was 1979, and we were farming. Questions popped up. What do you do if the manure spreader doesn't spread? Or the barn cleaner doesn't clean? And the milk machine doesn't milk? The same answer was found to all these questions. I said, "Fix 'em!"

The first month was really more of an orientation time for us, but the cold weather—27 degrees below zero—is what complicated matters and made them worse. We looked back at it as if it was like boot camp and were sure glad when it was over!

Our house was spacious. With spring in the air, I was busy cleaning and painting rooms. There was a large family room and a living room, with the kitchen tucked in between the two. Jeff and Jeremy were happy on the farm. They had cats to play with every day. And as the weather became warmer, they were outside a lot with me. The birth of a calf was a new experience for them. Although they didn't know or understand all the basics of a new life, it was an exciting time for them.

September 29th found me on the way to Appleton to Happy Joe's restaurant where we celebrated Richard's birthday. If at all possible, I would bake a birthday cake and be with each of my children on their birthdays.

Because our farm house had electric baseboard heaters in each room, which was a rather expensive way to heat, in October we had a neighbor install a large wood furnace in the basement. Having no heater of any kind in the basement made it really cold. Doing laundry in the basement after the installation was much more comfortable.

In November, our wedding attendants from Saukville came up to visit us and stayed a week. With a lot of woods around the farm, Harry and Milan went deer hunting. It was great to share the Thanksgiving meal together, which Virginia and I had prepared.

Our first Christmas on the farm held such excitement! The boys helped to get trimmings and decorations out that would be placed on the Christmas tree. As a family, we attended Wausau Bible Church, and the boys took part in the children's Christmas program. Later, we spent Christmas Eve with my family in Forest Junction, and then came back to Wausau in the wee hours of the morning on Christmas Day, bringing Lanetta with us.

December 29th, 1979 marked our first year on the farm. It was also a time to celebrate Milan's birthday with a party, and some of his relatives visited with us. The time flew by quickly as we enjoyed every day of being together.

A New Decade

It was the start-up of a new decade, the 1980s. For us, it was farming every day 24/7. In the beginning of the year, we rented a neighbor's barn to keep the heifers in, as our barn wasn't large enough to house them. This meant going every day, about a half mile down the road, to the neighbor's to feed and clean them out.

With work keeping us busy, time continued to fly by. I liked to bake, and with special days like Valentine's Day, heart cookies covered the entire kitchen table.

A month later, on March 15th, Lanetta turned seven years old. We chose Happy Joe's restaurant in Appleton as our party place, and eleven of her classmates were present. I so enjoyed being with them and baking her birthday cake!

Prior to attending the birthday party, I visited Grandpa Joseph Lingle in a Kaukauna nursing home. Many times, it felt like I was a roadrunner, going back and forth between families, a bit over one hundred miles one way, and then back again.

New projects seemed to keep surfacing. At the beginning of May, a neighbor boy who was helping us dug out an area for a sidewalk in front of the house. A few days later, cement was poured, completing a brand-new sidewalk! Just as it was on my first family farm, so it was going here; building—always building something new.

On May 30th, the silo builders came to erect a 20' x 70' Rochester concrete silo. It was finished on June 4th, ready for the first crop of hay. While my heart was throbbing with excitement, I ended up driving my husband to the emergency room, his finger badly cut by the hay chopper. Thankfully, he lost only one third of the finger! Our neighbor friends, Terry and Sue, came over and helped out with the work.

With the hay crop finally finished, it was on to the next undertaking. On August 8th, the milk house, which was old and not very big, was torn down. The following day we spent getting measurements, and readying the area to pour cement. After the floor was made firm and intact, block-laying began for the walls of our new milk house. By the middle of the month, it was completed. There it was; a new milk house, new roof, newly cemented floor, and a hallway with a new entrance into the barn.

The flip of the calendar saw Jeff off to his first day of school. He had to ride the high school bus, and then switch buses to attend the Wausau Christian School. A hired man (whose name was also Jeff) was staying with us and attending high school, so it was good to know "Big Jeff" looked out for "Little Jeff".

September was my son Richard's birthday month. We celebrated it one day before, on Sunday the 28th, by having a family dinner at Ponderosa restaurant in Appleton. It was another full day for me, arriving home at 12:45 am.

With fall here, I could be found busy canning applesauce, digging out carrots, bringing squash in, or finishing up other garden work. Barn windows were washed so the winter sun could later shine through, bringing with it the warmth that it shed. Cleaning and baking seemed to be my lot, more so in fall and winter.

Milan and I interacted with church folks, inviting them over for dinner many times after church. In December, a lot of Christmas cookies were baked and I gave most of them away as gifts, though I did keep enough for our family as well.

Each year, I remembered relatives and friends by sending them a Christmas letter, which kept me busy for a couple of days, sharing the love of Jesus in the observance of His birth.

We went to the Forest Junction farm on Christmas Day, and back home by 3:00 in the morning! We only slept a few hours before heading out to the barn to milk. An afternoon nap that day was greatly welcomed!

My Story: Faith, Family, Farm
1981

As 1981 made its entry, we made plans for the New Year. On January 12th, we signed papers to purchase a 20' x 60' Harvestor. This would be a sealed storage structure which would store the high-moisture corn and replace cob corn stored in a crib. Eleven acres of land had been cleared by a contractor. The job had started last fall and was finished up in spring, just in time for the planting of corn.

Things were going well until May 14th, when misfortune came to my husband. He broke his ankle as he planted corn on the newly cleared land. This meant more responsibility for me.

As he rested, the purchase papers signed in January were becoming a reality now, as the Harvestor crew came on May 26th. Thankfully, I usually had some help, and by May 29th, Milan had a walking cast put on, enabling him to get around. The foundation was finished on June 5th, now ready for the building crew to come.

Things were moving fast, and on June 11th, the Harvestor sheets were going up (the structure is built from the bottom, and jacked up 60 feet in the air). The "Big Blue" Harvestor was completed on June 15th, and the un-loader installed, ready for use!

On July 25th, Mary and her fiancé, Tom, came for a visit. They were looking at farms for sale in our area, and there was one available a couple miles from us. *Wouldn't that be great*, I thought, *if that would come to pass?* We could work together!

We had some drainage tiling done across the road from the farm by two men, sometimes three. They ate the noon meal with us each day they worked. It seemed there were always folks over for meals; good thing I didn't mind baking and cooking.

Talking about food preparation, with September came Labor Day. My husband's family came for a visit over the long weekend, and I baked eight pies, plus homemade bread. The oven wasn't resting!

Saturday night was pizza night, which the kids enjoyed. Sunday was a brat fry, along with hot dogs and our home-grown sweet corn. On Labor Day, we served fried chicken with all the trimmings. Certainly, it was a well-rounded, fun-packed weekend!

Later that month, on September 29th, I was on the way to the farm with a specially baked birthday cake for Richard. I spent so many trips going there that my car almost knew the way toward the Forest Junction farm by itself!

In October, our garden work was complete, and it had been an excellent season. I froze a lot of broccoli, green beans, and corn. This meant "good eating" through the cold winter months, and then some.

Being thankful for a great crop year, my husband's sister and children shared in our special thanks on Thanksgiving Day. They stayed overnight with us, and left the next day.

The month of December brought baking cookies, cookies, and more cookies! Baking gingerbread men, white sugar, cutout cookies, along with bars, homemade candies, and for sure fudge, kept me very busy! Everyone who received my bakery as a gift seemed to appreciate it.

1982

The beginning of the New Year came in with severely cold and blustery weather, which continued to get colder. On January 10th, the chill factor was way below zero, at 89 degrees below! Schools, church services, and any other meetings and activities were cancelled. Those were days we bundled up tight to do the farm work.

Milan and I had been invited to a banquet in February in recognition of our farm being chosen for the "Outstanding Young Farmer Award." This was a special event for us. The evenings had different speakers, and our pictures were taken and published in the local papers. We even stayed over at the Holiday Inn in Wausau.

I drove to Appleton to celebrate Lanetta's birthday at Happy Joe's as usual. Then, the week before Easter, I had Grandma Stanelle (my ex-husband's mom) and Lanetta with us. The whole family ate Easter dinner together, and later in the afternoon, they left for home with Mary and Tom, who were planning for their "big day"—their wedding on May 23rd. It was arranged then that I'd have to go down on April 30th to help do the wedding invites, which I did. It was one full day! I drove there early in the morning and was home in the wee hours of the next morning for milking time.

May 23rd arrived, and finally it was time for a wedding day! My brother came for the wedding; he had come into town two days earlier and stayed overnight by us. The boys and I went along with him to the Forest Junction farm to help out with last minute details. Milan drove down after the morning chores for the ceremony. Mary looked beautiful in her gown and the weather was perfect that day!

Oh, how I enjoyed summer, watching the garden grow in expectation of all the coming vegetables! Even amidst all the work needing to be done, I still took time to plant flowers. I believe flowers are "God's embroidery" showing off their beauty when they are in full bloom.

On June 15th, I received a phone call telling us Grandpa Lingle had died. Two days later, our family drove to the memorial service in Kaukauna. It was a time when relatives on my dad's side of the relation all got to visit together. Though I was sad for Grandpa's passing, I enjoyed seeing all of my cousins.

There was a family reunion in July for my mom's side of the relation. It was always held at the Stanelle Homestead, Grandfather's house. The boys and I went there for the noon meal; we visited for a while and returned home for the evening chores and milking.

August 8th was a vacation day for Milan and me. We asked a neighbor to do the evening milking so we could leave for Wisconsin Dells after the morning milking and chores. We really enjoyed ourselves, especially on the boat tour! After spending almost all day at the Dells, we went to visit Mary and Tom, who lived about a 45-minute drive away in Bear Valley. It was Tom's birthday, and after visiting with them for a while, we headed home, exactly at midnight.

Labor Day weekend again brought a visit from my husband's family. Milan's mom and stepdad, his brothers and sisters, and their families, all stayed with us. That weekend, we had around eighteen people staying in our six-bedroom home. The food included our home-grown sweet corn, fried chicken that we had catered in, and all the extra side dishes I prepared. Everyone really enjoyed spending time on the farm, and we enjoyed having them!

When it worked out, I wanted to spend time with my children on their birthdays, and so it was, this year I was out at the Forest Junction farm for Richard's birthday on September 29th. This time, I made lasagna, and of course, his birthday cake as well. On the way there, we picked up Grandpa Matt so he could enjoy celebrating with us. We left the party at 10:45 PM, took Matt to his Kaukauna home, and arrived on our farm at 1:30 AM, once again in the wee hours of the morning. We certainly lived the previous day to its fullness!

In October, I started to receive phone calls from Robert Jr. that he wasn't feeling well. He was experiencing double vision and dizziness. We made arrangements to have him seen at the Marshfield Clinic in Marshfield, Wisconsin. I went to get him on November 16th, and the following morning, we left early for his appointment. He had many tests while he was there, with no immediate results known. Later, we received word that the diagnosis pointed toward multiple sclerosis, a disease that attacks the central nervous system.

In December, Robert Jr. came up by us and wanted to see our family doctor. After multiple x-rays were taken, with the symptoms as they were, our doctor told us all indications were significant for multiple sclerosis. This was on December 13th, and the reality of his physical condition was to be accepted.

While Robert Jr. was dealing with the reality of his condition, the following weekend we were notified that "Grandpa" Matt had died. His funeral service was on December 21st in Kaukauna. We left after the morning work, and then went home again for evening chores. It was a sad day for me. He'd been such a kind man.

Several days later, our family left the farm after chores for our Christmas Eve family get-together at the Forest Junction farm. We opened gifts, had lunch, and didn't return home until 3:15 AM on Christmas Day!

After several hours sleep, we milked the cows, and then had the excitement of opening our own family gifts as we watched each other unwrap and savor what was inside each one. We then enjoyed the turkey dinner together that I had prepared.

As if all these events and driving weren't enough, on December 27th, Mary asked me to come help her clean her home. We painted the walls and ceilings in the bedrooms. I returned home late on the evening of the 28th. Needless to say, I was exhausted!

1983: My Turn

The year 1983 brought an experience in which it was "my turn". After caring for the boys with their colds and sore throats, a husband with a broken ankle and one third of a finger cut off, I was now in the hospital for a surgery. I was scheduled at 8:00 AM on January 9th for a total hysterectomy. My hospital stay lasted ten days. So many people from the church and my family came to visit me! Our family appreciated the many people that brought food to the house throughout my hospitalization, and even while I was home on bed rest for some time.

What a blessing to have good neighbors and friends! A neighbor friend, Sue, would come over and help the boys get ready and off to school. The last Sunday in January, my first venture out since surgery was to church. On that same day, Noris, our new hired man, started. We began milking three times a day at the end of January. There were always young neighbor guys over helping out, too, many times staying overnight. Slowly, I got back into the routine work of meals to be made, cleaning, laundry, etc. The first time being back at work in the barn, though, was one month after my surgery.

On Sunday, March 13th, we spent the day at Happy Joe's in Appleton for Lanetta's birthday party. It was a one-day trip, and Sherry, a neighbor girl, came along with me. The boys stayed home to help their dad with barn work. I appreciated that time with Lanetta.

Springtime presents itself in all its new life in nature. It is an exciting and busy time on the farm: seeding in the fields, cleaning up the yard, raking all the leaves that have fallen on the lawn...it was a lot of work to keep the place looking nice.

Milking three times a day ceased in the first week of May. The extra work was too much, with corn planting and all the barn chores that needed to be done. Besides, there's the saying, "All work and no play makes Jack a dull boy." And so, it was nice to have, across the road from our farm, a large pond where we could spend time away from work "agoin' fishing". As the boys grew older, they were allowed to go there without their dad. They'd catch walleye, perch, and pan fish, which we had added to the pond. Sometimes, they'd bring the fish home for me to cook, which turned out to be quite tasty.

1983: Accused

Robert Jr. was having difficulties with his physical condition. He called me on May 6th to tell me that he'd gone to Arizona. I didn't get any details about it all. Ten days later, I received another phone call from him; he was in the Calumet County Jail, accused of sexual assault. The following day, I drove to the county court house for a preliminary hearing for him, where he was ordered to spend fifteen days at the Winnebago Health Center.

Thoughts raced through my mind. *What is this really all about?* I went to visit him in the evening, then returned the following day, staying overnight with Lanetta. Then it was back to my family in Wausau.

There was garden planting, cutting the lawn for the first time that year, all keeping me busy and my mind occupied on things I didn't know *how* to think about. Robert Jr. couldn't offer any answers, either.

May rounded off to be quite a month. The 27th was Richard's high school graduation. I attended the party at the farm, where relatives, neighbors and friends spent time together congratulating Richard on his achievement. Staying overnight allowed me to visit the next day with Robert at the Health Center. From there, it was back home again.

The summer months were full, with routine house and barn work, garden, and lawn care. On July 17th, Lanetta and Robert Jr. both came up by us, via the bus. Robert Jr. stayed for four days and returned home by bus. Lanetta stayed longer.

In the end of July, Mary asked me to help her with cleaning projects. It was a three-hour drive to their farm; usually I drove down one day and was back home the next. This worked out well, as it gave me more time to visit with her. The last Sunday of July, we had our family reunion again. Milan, the boys, and I attended. Our hired hand did the evening milking for us so we could enjoy time with my extended family.

The garden gave us plenty of food. With such a large yield, it kept me busy canning pickles, freezing broccoli and beans, and soon after, sweet corn. And oh, the zucchini, which was a favorite! I'd bake delicious chocolate zucchini cake for dessert as often as I could.

The news surfaced that Robert Jr. had been accused by his now ex-wife of sexual assault of a minor. He had a hearing on August 8th, where he pled not guilty. Things continued to escalate for him, and he was still struggling with his deteriorating physical condition.

In October, he went to the City of Faith Hospital in Tulsa, Oklahoma for thirteen days. All indications proved he did indeed have multiple sclerosis, although he wasn't able to accept it as such.

A new month, November, was showing on the wall calendar. The weeks went by fast, leading up to deer hunting time and Thanksgiving Day. The day before Thanksgiving, Robert Jr. and Lanetta came up again on the bus. I made the traditional turkey dinner, with the annual treat of potato dumplings, all the extras, and pumpkin and mincemeat pies. Robert owned several businesses, and had many employees. Later in the afternoon, one of Robert's former employees came up to take him home. Due to his failing vision and a car accident in August, it had been deemed unsafe for him to drive anywhere.

The Tuesday after Thanksgiving day, my husband and I took Lanetta home. After the boys went off to school, we left at nine in the morning and returned just in time for chores and milking. Such was repeated many times when Lanetta would come to visit. How well I remember the tears as they rapidly rolled down my cheeks on the way home without her. Those were some of the toughest moments, not being able to spend every day with all of my children.

With Christmas around the corner, I planned all of the preparations to be done in between the regular routine work. But on December 5th, Milan had surgery on his left knee, which meant I was milking cows from here on out by myself for a while. We had a helper though, which I was thankful for, so I didn't have to do all the work myself.

December 12th, 1983 was a very unpleasant day for me as a mother. Robert Jr. was sentenced to three years at the State Prison in Waupun for sexual assault. I had traveled to the county court house to be present for it all. With everything that had been happening in my life, I constantly looked to the Lord for His strength. Knowing soon we'd be observing the coming of Jesus into our sin-cursed world, I had no one else to turn to, no one else that understood and really *knew* me, or knew all that had gone on and was going on in my life. No time for tears now. I had to carry on and get busy cleaning and re-arranging the family room for our Christmas tree.

Despite Robert Jr.'s circumstances, it was a good time together as we went next door to our neighbors' Christmas tree farm to pick out the tree that we wanted. My husband cut it down, and we brought it home in the farm truck. It was set up in its stand in the house, and the rest was up to me to get it trimmed.

On December 24th, just the boys and I went to the family farm in Forest Junction. We opened our presents, had lunch together, and got back home in the evening around seven o'clock, just in time to help finish work in the barn.

The month of December 1983 went out with sub-zero temperatures. It was below zero for several days. The barn, where our heifers were kept, froze badly! Realizing we had to make a change, and after four days of continually thawing and fixing water pipes and drinking cups, all the heifers were brought home. Such were the extra challenges on the farm!

Becoming a Caregiver

As we completed our fifth year on our farm here in Wausau, 1984 was making its entrance. A new year, a new month, and what a month it would be!

It seemed as if my life was on auto-pilot! With Robert Jr. now in the State Prison, I had to deal with all aspects of his business. He'd had me appointed as his power of attorney before his stay in Waupun. I really didn't feel qualified; nevertheless, I didn't refuse the responsibility. Eight different times, trips were made to visit Robert, and to clean out his office and apartment.

My husband and I, and our helper at the time, took our truck and hauled out all the large items: the desks, chairs, tables and filing cabinets. The car was loaded with all the smaller things. Robert's business partner took care of the appliances that would need to be returned, since Robert owned an appliance franchise. I visited with officers, attorneys and Robert Jr.'s accountant in handling the many loose ends of it all.

Plus, friends of ours, Karen and Bud, who were with New Tribes Missions, were getting ready to leave the country. They didn't have all their paperwork, or have permission to leave yet. Their house was already sold, and now being detained, it worked out for them to live with us for two weeks. How great!

Karen did the baking (to this day her sweet roll recipe is a favorite of ours) and the cleaning, and her husband, Bud helped my husband outside. All the while, I was involved with Robert Jr.'s situation.

February found us getting equipment cleaned out of Bob's Dairy, which was a BouMatic dairy equipment and supply company, operated and owned by Robert Jr., alongside of his appliance franchise.

On the evening of March 2nd, we received a phone call from Waupun Prison. Robert Jr. had been taken to the University Hospital in Madison. Several hours later, the hospital called and informed us that he was, in fact, there. Because he'd been just admitted, there was little information they would give to me.

Two days later, on Sunday, I left to visit Robert Jr. in Madison. I stayed there for a couple of hours, then left for Mary's to visit with her, since she and her husband didn't live far from Madison. Robert Jr. was in the hospital for nine days, under medical supervision for his MS, before he returned to Waupun.

On Lanetta's birthday, I first went to visit Robert Jr., and on the way back, I stopped by to see Lanetta after she got home from school. I brought a Kentucky Fried dinner for us all to enjoy together, plus her birthday cake. Fortunately, Milan had a helper and the boys, so he wasn't left alone with all the farm work.

A few weeks later, on the third weekend in April, I took off to Waupun again to visit Robert Jr. On the way home, I stopped by the Forest Junction farm to pick up Lanetta. She traveled back with me so she could spend Easter vacation with us. Jeff's birthday was the day after Easter. We had a large party for him, with neighbor friends and classmates over at our house. It was hard to believe he was nine years old, and Lanetta, eleven years old already.

May 13th came with the exciting news that Mary had given birth to her first baby, my fourth grandchild, a baby boy named Dwayne. The following day, I drove down to Reedsburg Hospital, near Madison, to welcome Mary into the new realm of "motherhood" and to see the new arrival. I couldn't hold him, as back then babies were kept separate in the infant nursery, and could only view him through the glass.

The phone rang on June 21st, and the person on the other end of the line informed me of Robert Jr.'s parole. In previous conversations, I had asked for clemency due to his physical condition, and it was granted. A parole officer came to our home, and it was agreed upon by them and our family that Robert Jr. would stay with us for a while. At the time, I didn't realize what a long journey we'd have ahead of us.

So, on June 28th, I left to get Robert Jr., whose physical condition had gotten much worse. Within the month of July came numerous trips to see medical professionals, as I was the one who took him to our family doctor and chiropractor in Wausau.

At the end of July, our family—my husband, the two boys, and I—took a day vacation. We left early after milking and chores, traveling up north. We visited a game farm, rode horses, took a boat ride, and saw a lot of nature's beauty. All that, and we were still back home in time to do the evening farm work.

August was a busy month, with the regular chores; plus, we were pickling pickles, and canning and freezing beans. Robert Jr. was still with us and the doctor visits were less often. Things were beginning to become routine in caring for him. His vision had become worse. He could still walk, but had a very unsteady gait. All in all, he had settled in with our family; another plate at the table was always welcome, with extra laundry and caregiving in general.

Jeremy celebrated his golden birthday on the 8th of September. He had a party at our home, with neighborhood friends and some classmates.

Lawn cutting was a regular project, which the majority of the time I did. There was always something to be done; my life was a *whirlwind* of living! The corn harvest was in "full gear" during October; chopping silage in the silos and combining corn for in the Harvestor. The garden work was ending; the last of the carrots were dug out. Our first hard frost of the season came on October 30th, with the thermometer showing 28 degrees. Another growing season had ended.

Lanetta was able to stay with us the last week of October, having school vacation those days. My car seemed to be like a taxi—taking the boys to the dentist and Jeremy to Boy Scouts. Both boys were in football at school, which meant picking them up after practice, as well as watching them play at their local games.

Deer hunting time crept up fast! My brother-in-law and one of his friends came up and stayed with us for the hunting season. Most often, someone successfully bagged a deer. Much of the meat was then made into sausage. For Thanksgiving dinner that year, it was just our own family (Dad, Mom, the boys, and Robert Jr.). We still had our special meal of turkey, dressing, and all the trimmings.

By December, an appointment was made for Robert Jr. at the Mayo Clinic in Rochester, Minnesota. He and I traveled to Mary's on the 8th, stayed overnight, and left early in the morning to be at his appointment at the clinic. Robert Jr. ended up staying at the hospital, and I left for home. After being hospitalized for five days, he came back by plane to Central Wisconsin Airport, where we picked him up.

The year was drawing to a close, with all the extra Christmas events; the boys' school and church programs, along with the family get-togethers. We attended my husband's family's Christmas party, which was held in Neenah. It seemed like we were always going somewhere.

Another Year Goes By

January 7th brought another birthday for Mary. With a birthday cake in my hands, I left after the morning work was completed, driving down to spend part of her special day with her.

Several days later, I went with Milan to a farm auction in the area. He bought a wash rack to place inside our milk house, which is in there yet today.

The middle of January brought an 80-degree sub-zero chill factor. Work on the farm was very intense at this time! The cold affected everything; chains became stiff, tractors didn't want to start, and the cows' drinking cups froze, which would require us to thaw them out with hot water. If needed, a propane heater was used.

The church services we attended were telecast through the local television station. Jeff and Jeremy sang in the Lamplighters choir, which was telecasted on the last Sunday of the month. They thought it was "cool" to see themselves on television!

On February 20th, I received news that Granny Stanelle (my mother-in-law) had died. Our family all went to the memorial service held in Forest

Junction on the 23rd. She was in a nursing home at the time of her death, so it was just Richard, Lanetta, and their dad on the farm now. Mary had been married and gone from the farm several years already, so I met a few times with a local attorney to look into having Lanetta live with us.

March came in "like a lion" and we received over ten inches of snow with cold temperatures! It was the regular routine schedule of work throughout March. The month went by fast!

In the beginning of April, I drove down to Mary's to get Lanetta, who had been staying with her sister for a while. She was with us until Easter Sunday, and in the afternoon, I took her halfway and met Bob, who took her home with him.

The day after Easter, Robert Jr.'s ex-wife brought their two boys, Evan and Eric, up to visit with us. My husband took all the boys fishing on the river. On one occasion, Eric fell in the water and Jeff had to rescue him. Those were some tense moments! The boys stayed with us for four days, and then returned home to Appleton by bus.

The beauties of nature unfolded; it was May, with flowering trees, tulips and more, and it was time for the seeds to be planted in the ground. Milan was busy planting crops, as I was looking to plant the garden again, and flowers, too.

June seemed to be "dentist month". I had a couple of appointments to get two teeth crowned. The boys had their exams, and cavities filled. Lanetta was with us at the time, so she also came along to have her teeth checked. There were doctor appointments, too, for Robert Jr. as well. It was never a dull moment between the work and my involvement with the children.

Family reunion time was held the last Sunday of July. Lanetta came along with us and stayed for summer vacation. Then, in August, it meant "back to school" sales. Summer would soon be winding down, with the routine of school days resuming.

A new farm undertaking was started in October. My husband had trees cut down in our woods and had them taken to the local saw mill, where they were cut into logs to be used in the building of a farm workshop. The workshop was being built by us, not a contractor; my husband's friend who was a builder spearheaded the project.

The building was 30' x 40'. By the beginning of November, the roof was put on. When that was completed, the cement floor was poured on the following day. We were glad when it was finished, since the cold weather was settling in the first week in December.

There was a blustery snow storm, and school was called off for two days. As I looked out the window, viewing the cold, sullen stillness of the winter scene, tears filled my eyes. It was a time of reflection for me as I reviewed all the happenings in my life over the past years.

Never one to sit still for long, the farm work went on as usual. I squeezed in time to decorate the house and get ready for our Christmas observance. Soon, another year would become history.

No Such Thing as Unemployment

In 1986, Robert Jr.'s health continued to worsen. We took him to a different health center, and his dad came up to visit him in the beginning of the New Year. Robert Jr. stayed in the health center for only a couple of weeks. The conditions were such that we, as a family, agreed he would be better off living with us. Through our family doctor, arrangements were made to bring him back home.

There was never a dull moment on our farm! My favorite saying was, "There is no such thing as unemployment here!" Work goes on, 24/7.

Milan and I went on a fast trip to an auction held in the area where Mary lived. On the way home, we stopped to visit them and see their new daughter, Shannon, born on March 12th. Their farm was a three-hour drive from us, about 160 miles, so in one day it was a fast trip!

Jeremy, Robert Jr., and I helped Lanetta celebrate her birthday with a party at—you guessed it—Happy Joe's. Driving there and back equaled a full day! She'd come to visit us via bus now, which meant less travel for me to get her and take her back to Forest Junction.

Another season of planting and harvesting came again...and the year went on. In between crops and caring for the cows, my husband was busy with the electric wiring in the newly built shop. Family reunion time, birthdays, and holidays were all special family times to be remembered. The calendar schedule was always filled up with some activity or meeting.

Winter in many ways was welcomed that year. It allowed more time to work on things in the house. I'd catch up on sewing, cleaning out drawers, and paperwork, etc. February was tax time, with our bookkeeping done monthly. I gave all the month's business to our Farm Credit Agency, and they had it all computerized for us.

Richard had come to visit us the last week in February. He was not living at home with his dad now, as he had taken on work at a prominent Guernsey dairy farm in Onalaska. We enjoyed our time with him.

Spring was approaching with all the newness in nature. It was always a thrill to hear the honking of the geese and see them in their formation in the sky. It was confirmation that spring was here! Noise of the tractors revving up would soon be heard, with another planting season upon us.

An elderly neighbor of ours, a man who was contemplating getting rid of his milk cows, came over and talked to my husband about it. Milan said he would help him if he wanted to keep his milk cows, even though he was busy himself with the crop work, just finishing up the corn planting.

Milan remembered our wedding anniversary, May 13th, and together we went out to eat at a fine restaurant in Wausau. A good deal on a 24-foot swimming pool caught our attention. The hot weather, which we knew would be coming soon, made it all too inviting to look at. Not ones to dally, we purchased the pool and set it up in the back of the house. It was ready for water, so our milkman came with his milk truck to fill it up for us.

The boys beat me, going in the pool first. I followed after them. How refreshing it was in the hot, humid weather! The pool meant extra work, keeping it vacuumed clean, and adding the solutions that the test kit called for. It was worth it for the enjoyment we got out of it!

In the middle of August, our family took a one-day trip to Onalaska to visit the farm where Richard was working. The owner gave us a tour of the farm and showed us his unique idea. He had an unused Harvestor that was converted into a calving pen, which I had never seen done before. It was a smart idea and a great utilization of space! Plus, there were no corners for the calves to get stuck in.

When school vacation ended, Jeff entered John Muir Middle School and Jeremy went to Riverview Elementary. They were growing up so fast!

They were two birthday boys in September. We had a party for Jeremy's eleventh birthday on the 8th, and he had friends over. Richard's birthday was the 29th. Again, my husband and I drove to Onalaska, bringing him his homemade birthday cake baked with "Mom's Love". The couple he worked for treated us to a big buffet dinner at the Bonanza Restaurant located right next to their farm. It was delicious.

Then, just a few days later—a news flash! On October 9th, another new grandbaby was born! Shianne Lurvey, a little girl, joined Tom and Mary's family. That made six grandchildren for me. I didn't feel that old; yet here I was, a grandmother!

Fall work was winding down; corn harvest nearing its end. I had all the geraniums dug out and put into flowerpots, ready to bring into the house. I would do this year to year, planting them back outside in the spring. The garden work was completed, awaiting the time for the ground to be covered with snow. It was a sure sign of what was ahead—winter!

November stood out as hunting time. My brother-in-law came for the week, but went back for Thanksgiving Day to be with his family, only to come back for the rest of the week for more hunting.

Baking was accelerated with December showing on the calendar; cookies and more cookies, with Christmas strudels, too. The aroma of the evergreen Christmas tree filled the house. Richard came to spend six days with us. Christmas Eve was spent together by Lanetta's, after which we returned back home in the wee hours of the morning. I so enjoyed Christmas time—the observance of the coming of Jesus into our world!

Jeffrey and Jeremy, in their Riverview flag football jerseys, 1985

Another Plate at the Table

Wow, it would be ten years now that we purchased our farm. Our family would be growing by one more this year. Richard had decided to go on to school, attending the University of Wisconsin-Extension in Wausau to study agriculture and dairy science. The second semester classes started on January 27th.

In the 1987-1988 school year, my children attended four different schools. Jeremy was in 6th grade in elementary school. Jeff was in 7th grade at the junior high school. Lanetta was in her first year of high school, and Richard began his first year at the UWMC. Robert Jr. was still with us; his condition physically was not getting better. The children sure kept me busy!

There was the season of planting again, and spring ran into summer, bringing with it the hot weather. It was a time when we could really enjoy the pool! That summer was very hot and dry; a drought had set in. It turned out to be a very slim harvest of crops.

It seemed that school no sooner let out for summer vacation when it started up again. Jeff and Jeremy were together in middle school now. Jeff was quarterback of the Red Team football squad. It was fun to watch the team win all of their games, but one. Jeremy played flag football with the seventh-grade team.

Richard would be finishing his final exams the week before Christmas. In January, he'd start his second semester at the University of Wisconsin in Madison. He'd made arrangements to live off campus with a former high school classmate.

Fall season saw its end and all the work and activities that went with it. Thanksgiving time and the Christmas season followed with all the usual extra baking, then gift buying, and sharing of good family times.

It was now 1989, the dawning of a new year. No way was I expecting what lay ahead!

Divorced

In February of 1989, a large semi-load of hay from out west pulled into our yard. Not being able to harvest much of our own hay crop due to the drought, hay had to be purchased. In March, Milan went to a nearby auction and bought the feed in the silo there. It meant every other day going with a wagon and getting feed for the cattle.

Previous to this, Milan had gone along with a neighbor to another auction where he had purchased two cows, one of which broke her leg while being unloaded off the trailer at our farm. Not good! We did what we had to do. The following day she was taken to a meat packing plant west of here.

It seemed the negatives of farming were stressing my husband out. He communicated less, would go away many times in the evenings, and not say where he was going. We continued to work on as usual, though at times the air seemed very tense. It was like our marriage was on life support!

My husband kept busy by planting the crops. His folks visited us in May to get their camper, which was stored in our shed. They came often, and several times would stay overnight.

The elderly man who had talked to my husband about keeping his cows looked for the extra help now. Milan helped him correct things in the barn so he could get a Grade A permit. Then, he started going over there to help the man milk. Come June, Milan would not come home from the neighbor's farm right after milking. Instead it was 1:30 or later in the morning by the time he'd crawl into bed. The boys and I would do the milking, calf feeding, and all the work at our place alone. He would be with young guys and girls at the old farm house there. The elderly man lived in a newer little house up by the road.

We did a lot of talking after I confronted my husband on June 19th. I asked him directly, "Do you want our marriage to work?" to which he replied, "No!" He'd never say why, though.

We didn't have marital problems, financial problems, or in-law problems. Being his helpmate with the farm work, doing the bookwork, baking, cleaning, wanting to do my best as a homemaker and as a mother to his children, I questioned it all. Just as a football coach pulls his team into the locker room to replay moments of the game, I tried to sort through all of our experiences together.

On June 28th, I wasn't told up front, but I found out that my husband had gone to an attorney and written a five-hundred-dollar retainer check. Now I knew; he was proceeding with divorce. He kept pulling away from me; gone a lot in the evenings, and even during some days between milking. At times, he wouldn't return at all, at which time the boys and I did all the work.

Milan left for California to visit his brother. Being gone for over a week, he never called or was in touch. Trying to surprise Milan upon his return, the boys and I cleaned up the feed room floor. In doing so, we found out later that the old silage had been acting as a ground for the electricity flowing through an extension cord on the floor. Removing the silage and exposing the cord resulted in a cow being electrocuted. We found her dead body lying on the ground with her neck on the elevator.

We called our electrician and he stated that cows are very susceptible to voltage; and it was a good thing it was a cow, and not one of us, who had touched it. The unseen caring of God was evident that day.

Meanwhile, we had a good harvest of crops. The silo filled with silage, more than enough hay, and high-moisture corn filled the Harvestor to capacity!

The boys and I went to church alone. For some time now, their dad hadn't attended with us. It was on Sunday, October 22nd, after arriving home from church, that we found out that he'd taken all his clothes and moved out! He did come back four days later and picked up the boys, and when they came back, he stayed a bit. There was very little talk between us, but he repeatedly came back, wanting to use me as his wife. Needless to say, it was an intensely emotional time for me!

In the past, I had purchased a small plaque with words of off-set printing on it. It is still sitting by my kitchen sink. As I re-read the words, I realized how much I needed them, for truly my needs were great! It reads:

"God said, 'Don't look to the bigness of your need. Look to the Bigness of your God. Your circumstances are hindrances to seeing My Abilities. If you keep your eyes on your circumstances, the devil will use them to defeat you, and accuse the Word of God, the written Word and the Living Word. Your victory is in keeping your eyes on the Bigness of your God, and His Abilities. He has promised to take you step by step by step, not all at once, but step by step...and Each Step will be a Miracle!'"

I knew God (not only about Him) through His Son, Jesus, whom I accepted as my Personal Savior on June 23rd, 1963. It seemed as I was taking baby steps, I was learning to trust God in everything! Life was too big for me; I couldn't handle it alone.

On Christmas Day, we had a wonderful family day together. My husband was with us. We had our gift exchange, with Jeff getting the only thing he wanted; a male Siamese cat he named Kelso. What a great pet he turned out to be! Milan spent the evening and overnight with me. We shared an evening of love, as if nothing could be wrong between us.

I'll never forget Milan's dazed look as he sat on our family room davenport the next day. I had to say good-bye; I so disliked good-byes!

After the morning milking by myself, I went to see my attorney to give him money for a settlement, at which time it would be taken to the court house. The divorce was finalized on December 26th, 1989. I didn't want to appear in the divorce proceedings, so arrangements were made and I signed a waiver of appearance. My attorney handled it all, and I was thankful for that. I was still in love with Milan, but I knew for the sake of the boys and me, I had to move on.

Marjorie M. Beyersdorf

Double M Faith Farm Logo, 1990s

A New Decade

Here it was, 1990, a new decade, a New Year with new experiences of farming without a husband, and the boys growing up without their dad around. Even though we'd been doing all the work ourselves for a couple months now, we realized this was the way it would be now—it was final. The boys wanted to stay on the farm, and their dad had no intentions for them to live with him. What a state of change and turmoil in my life! It was overwhelming to know the responsibilities were all on my shoulders.

More than ever, I realized the words in our farm prefix were not only words, but reality in action—Double M Faith Farm. Double M stood for Milan and Marjorie (now it stands for Marjorie May) and the word "faith" is from Hebrews 11:6 in the Bible: "Without faith it is impossible to please God, for he that cometh to God must believe that He is, and that He is a rewarder of those who diligently seek Him."

I relied heavily on God, and the many resources from people who helped us out. Our veterinarian, the feed nutritionist, our crop agronomist, and my lender were with us all along the way. Since my husband had taken care of all cow mating records, I wasn't sure which cows were pregnant, so new charts were made after having the veterinarian check each cow.

Then, a much-needed undertaking was getting a new ventilation system in the barn. A lot of moisture inside wasn't good for the cows. Wisconsin Public Service, the utility center, was consulted. They were in the process of evaluating fans, output, energy, etc. and they advised me they would install three 48-inch Acme fans and one 36-inch fan. These fans would pull fresh air from openings at the opposite end of the barn. This investment proved to be a great one, and there was no more moisture in the barn. It was more comfortable for the cattle and for us while we were working in there. How welcome, in the hot summer days, to have a two-and-a-quarter mile breeze flowing through the barn.

I had hired help for fieldwork, along with the boys. Jeff, who was fifteen years old now, was the dominant machinery man. (I can't help but think back to how he'd take our tractors apart and overhaul them.) Jeremy, who was fourteen, was the one who hand-fed the cows rations of salt, minerals, and high-moisture corn. He was also the main helper, along with me, in milking.

I was proud of the boys as they worked on the farm like men. Oftentimes, they'd have friends over, and their friends would help in with the work. Myself, I had become an "all-country girl" who enjoyed work; and had that not been, I could never have dealt with all that had been happening.

Robert Jr.'s physical condition continued to get worse and he was bedridden now. The Visiting Nurses Association came every day to bathe him and change the bed sheets. A registered nurse came once a week. Our doctor had said Robert Jr. was at an advantage living with us, rather than in a nursing home. Because I wasn't punching a clock, it worked out for me to care for my son. I did his laundry, fed him, and kept up his morale. It wasn't a hardship to care for him; he had a great attitude and a good sense of humor.

When Robert Jr. had left his business, he had a little Shih Tzu dog named Ginger, who came to live with us. Ginger had puppies, and we kept one of them, a little male we named Chumpie. These dogs gave us a lot of enjoyment, and they were great companions for Robert Jr. Yes, they were extra work, with having to take them to the groomers, letting them outside, etc., but they were worth it!

The year 1990 ended up being very productive. The crops were good, and the cows were doing well in production of milk. We were thankful to have one full-time and one part-time helper.

Marjorie M. Beyersdorf
The Early '90s

With one year of a new decade past, we looked forward to what the New Year, 1991, would bring. Jeff was in his second year of high school and Jeremy was in his first year. Jeff was active in Future Farmers of America, and together, we attended the FFA banquet. It was rather uneasy for me to be a boss and their mother all at the same time; however, we worked well together as a team.

An investment was needed this year; we felt it was time to upgrade the milking equipment. There was the purchase of four new automatic take-offs (which are the milking machines) and a total automatic sanitation wash system. In fall, two additional automatic take-offs were purchase, which meant one person could handle three machines on a row of cows. This worked out best, with two people milking, one on each side.

I attended two special events; one being when Richard graduated from the University of Wisconsin in Madison on May 19th. Being a country gal and not accustomed to big city driving, there were some hesitant moments for me while driving alone to the graduation ceremony. I did it though, and we spent a great day together!

Lanetta graduated from high school on June 2nd. There was a lot of food and drink at the Forest Junction Elementary School after the graduation exercise. There was the gathering of friends and relatives as we shared in celebration, and visiting with one another.

Then, it was summer, and what a busy time! The first hay field was chopped off and went into the silo on June 4th. With the corn all planted, now it was "waiting time" as we waited for it to grow.

One summer afternoon, a motorcycle drove into our yard, and riding on it was a North Central Technical School agriculture teacher from here in Wausau. He had found out that I was farming alone with the two boys and some hired help, and came to invite me to enroll in the Farm Business and Production Management classes held on Wednesday evenings.

I had to think that through. *How could I take on more work?* Somehow, some way, it would happen, and come time for classes to start, I was there! The boys would finish up the work on the farm and await my return, because, often times, I would bring tacos home from the nearby Taco Bell. There were times I'd receive calls from them during class or break with issues such as, "Mom, we're out of water" or "The dog just puked by the deck door. When are you coming home?" I would've replied, "I'll be home as soon as I can after class" and in regards to the dog puke, "Well, clean it up!"

As I look back now, I'm so happy I did attend. The learning in class, as well as discussions with fellow and gal students, was all so very helpful. I realized just being a helpmate on the farm was sure different than now being "behind the steering wheel" myself!

It was a good feeling to have the silo full of silage and dry hay in the barn, enough for our winter feeding. The guys were busy combining corn, and soon all the harvesting would be finished. I cleaned up the garden (I never did any fieldwork), and my specialty was with the cows. I kept breeding records, herd health, feed inventory, and all the bookkeeping in general.

Due to financial margins being tight on the farm, a new venture started on February 3rd, which would be a way we could increase income without much extra expense in order to help our bottom line. We milked the dairy herd three times a day instead of two; eight o'clock in the morning, four o'clock in the afternoon, and at midnight. I loved the midnight milking! Many times, as I'd finish up in the wee hours of the morning, the birds would be starting their morning songs. I'd say to them, "Hey birds, we've got to sleep. Keep the volume low."

In between all the routine work, we stayed busy cleaning up around the farm. A Universal milking equipment tour, sponsored by Dave's Dairy, brought other farmers out to see our farm set-up and the complete milking system.

Another tour in spring came, with Double M Faith Farm hosting *Food for America*. This was an annual event where fourth grade students from the Wausau Public School system were taken by bus to a different farm each year. The high school students of Future Farmers of America do all the work in setting up different area stations on the farm to explain and teach agriculture. My son, Jeff, was president of that organization at Wausau East High School during that time.

Life on the farm was *really* 24/7 now! With milking every eight hours, all other work in between, plus the special events held on the farm, it brought me to know that "The busy person is the one that gets things done!"

The boys and our hired hand were kept busy planting corn and soybeans. We had rented some additional land to plant crops on, besides our own. All crops were used as feed for the cows. No additional feed had to be purchased. As the field work wound down, we took a day off and spent it on Lake Wausau. With our small motor boat purchased from neighbors "Uncle" Don and "Aunt" Ede, we went fishing; and although the fish weren't cooperating in taking the bait, it was still a fun day! We used our own worms, picked in the yard, and the boys even sold some to others for five cents apiece.

In June, Robert Jr. entered the hospital for some minor surgery. He was there one day short of a week. Lanetta came up on the bus for three days in July. Her trips weren't as frequent now, as she was involved more at home and working at the Forest Junction Cafe. Richard and his friend, Patti, visited over the summer; it was always good to be together and stay in touch.

Then there was an unexpected happening! A wagonload of hay bales tipped over, making extra work to get them all picked up.

The boys worked like men, but not always. In the farm workshop, they built a "hot rod car" out of an older model car. It was only driven off-road in our fields, though. Both boys had their own four-wheelers, too. Believe me, God's mercy and grace and His protection were abundantly present! The boys were still boys, and along with their friends, very adventurous!

As usual, the year would soon be past in the annals of time. Fall work was completed, and we were thankful for all the crops. We ate healthy, homegrown veggies as we enjoyed a Thanksgiving turkey dinner. Right on the heels of Thanksgiving, Christmas season came. When its observance was over, a new calendar was put on the wall.

1993

Enter the New Year, 1993. It was hard to believe we had completed two full years of successful farming. Had it not been for the boys, I would have become a farm workaholic!

But for God's mercy and grace, I could never have dealt with the many happenings in my life alone. At times, I felt like just wiping it all away and locking the door of my heart and life!

The routine activities continued to be carried out. I was attending agriculture night classes at the technical college every Wednesday night. Farm work was always there. The boys helped in the morning before going to school by feeding the cows. I would do the milking, and feed the baby calves.

Robert lived with us, and the doctor and visiting nurses determined it would be best to come every day. They said they enjoyed coming to the farm to take care of Robert, and see all its activities going on. Despite him being bedridden, I'm thankful his spirits were kept up. He didn't have a depressed attitude. People would ask me different questions like, "Isn't he a burden to care for?" But I would answer, "It makes me all the more thankful that I have health and strength to get up each morning. I never take it for granted!"

In February, Richard told me he wanted to make arrangements to fly out to Arizona and take me to visit my brother. I had never been to visit him, and this would be my first airplane ride, too. We left on March 2nd and returned on the 7th.

My brother took us to big farms in the area, one of which was named Shamrock Farm, and which had 10,000 cows! I had never seen anything in my life like that! We went into Tucson, and on the way visited a white cathedral. The steakhouse we ate at, called Monty's Steakhouse, was known for its delicious steaks. They gave us all the nacho chips and salsa we wanted; that's the first time I ever ate that. We also visited a cactus garden. Every day we were going somewhere and doing something.

The boys and hired help did an excellent job in doing all the work on the farm while I was gone. After all the crop planting was finished, we looked forward to a big day for Jeff. His last year in high school completed, it resulted in a graduation celebration on June 8th. Lanetta was working in her dad's restaurant, and catered most of the food. A tent was set up outside, and friends, classmates, and neighbors came, and we all had a good time.

Summer kept the boys busy with the hay crop. For myself, again working in the garden, there was a lot of routine yard work, grass cutting, etc.

Fall came, and it wasn't only house cleaning time, but barn cleaning also. We hired whitewashers that came and did all the cleaning. In October, we hosted a barn meeting for students enrolled in agriculture night class at the North Central Technical College. The evening was videotaped, and a copy was given to me as a memento of our class night spent together on the farm.

The brisk fall air meant the cold nights would be approaching. This time of year, we would be getting wood to throw down to the basement. There wasn't a lot of wood on hand, and the decision was made to have an oil furnace installed. The amount of time to make wood (which our time in farm work didn't allow, rather than hire it out) justified the decision to purchase the oil furnace.

A few weeks later, dreaming of a white Christmas wasn't a dream. The ground was all white, covered with its sparkling blanket of snow. Christmas in the air always meant an extra busy time with all the preparations. Family time, as all came together for Christmas Eve, was a wonderful time in our home. With the excitement of giving and receiving gifts, we remembered the Greatest Gift of all: Eternal Life in Jesus as told in the Bible in Romans 3:23.

Marjorie M. Beyersdorf
The Good, the Bad, and the Messy

In the beginning of the New Year, 1994, reality set in; we installed the new heating furnace in our house. It was a better investment to go with a new energy efficient one. With the turn of the thermostat, how great it was to have a warm house again! It seemed so easy compared to having to keep wood in the stove, besides all the work to get the wood.

January brought the birth of my seventh grandchild, Sierra Lynn, Tom and Mary's fourth child. There were now four granddaughters and three grandsons.

Having no hired help at this time, my eyes were constantly searching in the agriculture newspaper and Country Connections to find someone. Several contacts were made from different men, persons who came to the farm, but who seemed to only want a place to "hang their hat". Plus, they were interested in me as a gal! I was merely looking for someone to help the boys on the farm. Marriage was not an option at the time.

I remember all too well, one fellow who hauled out the manure with the tractor and manure spreader. In cleaning the barn, the spreader was filled to the top. Because of his inability in shifting the tractor, resulting in it jerking, the manure slopped from one end to the other and over the top, spilling out on the road. Someone on a motorcycle drove by, getting full of it. The police were called and we were engaged in cleaning up the blacktop road. And I had just wanted "help" to come alongside of the boys!

Jeff, being out of high school, took the reins of the field and tractor work. Classmates of Jeff's would often come by to be of help, as well as just to spend time on the farm with us.

News came from Lanetta that she had purchased a dairy supply building owned by Robert Jr. in Forest Junction and was having it remodeled into a restaurant, making her dream come true of owning her own restaurant. The experience of her working in a nearby place for over five years proved to be an inspiration and a great asset to her.

But not all was well at home. Because of Robert being constantly in bed, he developed bed sores, and they were becoming a problem. He needed to be taken to the hospital for special treatments several times. Keeping up with all this just seemed to be my lot in life!

Toward summer's end, I was approached by a representative of Purina Feeds. They asked if we would be willing to host the celebration of Purina's one hundredth birthday on our farm. We felt it to be an honor! Along with our dairy herd nutritionist, we set out to make plans.

The event started at 7:00 PM with a farm tour, directed by our dairy supply personnel. A program was held in our workshop, and the topics that were presented were about health products, proof of income/over feed costs, and aggressive reproduction. A luncheon for everyone included a very large birthday cake (all furnished by Purina), which completed the evening.

Happy Occasions

It was 1995, and as each year dawns anew, with it comes change and new experiences. This year would be no different.

On January 2nd, Lanetta held the opening day of her new restaurant, the Forest Junction Café, which quickly became well attended. There was a large seating room for at least 50 people, and stools by the counter. She would have Friday night and Sunday buffets, all home cooked and made from scratch. On special days like Mother's Day, there was a line of people waiting to eat. How exciting things were now, to look forward to the day when I'd be able to see her in her very own business!

Cabin fever? Not me. The months of February and March seemed to go by all too fast. Regular work, tax meetings, appointments with the crop agronomist, and the making of our farm and home plans were all taking up my time. Also, in these months, I liked to clean kitchen cupboards, knowing when the weather warmed up, come April, work became much longer outside.

I received a wedding invite in March, and it was a day I eagerly awaited. On April 1st, Richard and Patti were to be married. The wedding took place in Seymour, Wisconsin, the city they'd call home. It was a great day of family celebration!

The robins were back, and with them, the fresh smell of the new grass growing, the trees all budding out. I knew soon the aroma of the lilacs and the apple tree blossoms would permeate the air. And that meant planting time; first the seeding of alfalfa, then soybeans, and the corn. The satisfaction of work completed now rested in the hands of God. He gives the rain and the sunshine, and He gives the increase. We can count on God and His promises. "As long as the earth remains, seedtime and harvest, and cold and heat, and summer and winter, and day and night shall not cease." A promise to count on from God's Word in Genesis 8:22.

Summer brought the usual full schedule of activity for me, with the garden and the flower beds all needing weeding and care, and also clipping the lawn. The boys, along with some of their friends who came to spend time on the farm, were busy doing the hay harvest. Not long after, as fall was approaching, it was time to chop corn silage into the silo. The remaining corn was custom combined, and put into the Harvestor high-moisture storage unit.

Time of Sorrow

On December 5th, Robert was taken to the hospital. He had developed a respiratory condition, making it hard for him to breathe. Visits to the hospital were every day for me. There wasn't much the doctors could do.

The day before his death, a nurse from the hospital called me and said, "I don't think Robert will live much longer, if you want to contact his children." The following day I proceeded to do just that. I phoned his ex-wife, and she came that same evening with their children. We had a time of visiting and prayer together. I was so very thankful that nurse had called me!

The following day, I spent several hours with him. Upon returning home for chores in the evening, I received the call from the hospital. After a week and one day in the hospital, my son, Robert Jr., had died. Robert's physical life was gone. What followed after Robert's death wasn't easy! The tasks of selecting a casket, writing up an obituary for the newspaper, and making arrangements for the body to be taken from the funeral home here in Wausau to the church in Forest Junction, where the memorial service would be held, all needed to be done.

I believe it was the mercy of God that He allowed Robert to be stricken with multiple sclerosis. Robert had been a very aggressive person, self-willed, and skilled in doing whatever he wanted to do, right or wrong, mostly not always right. God allowed him a lot of time to see himself as God sees him, and to realize that life is not in our own hands. Awhile after he had come up to stay with us, he sat on our family room davenport, crying like a baby. He knew in his heart that he needed God to forgive him, and so we prayed together.

At the memorial service, I gave a talk, sharing some of our experiences for the folks there. I also shared this poem:

My Story: Faith, Family, Farm

This Old Tent
By Steve Coyle

*When I looked upon the days gone past
I'd thought this tent was built to last.
For I'd stood it on some rocky ground
Where stormy winds couldn't beat it down.
And with much pride and my own hand,
I put my tent in shifting sand.
Where pegs pulled loose and my tent did shake
But I was young and I could take
The unstable world that I was in.
I'd just up and move again.
Then I put my tent out in the sun
Where it was warm and I had some fun.
Then the hot sun rays grew hotter yet
But I was strong, this was no threat.
So for many years I went this route;
Shifting this old tent about
Till one cold day when my mind grew clear.
This tent had an end and it might be near.
So with much fear, such a heavy load,
I looked for the one who made this abode.
Yes, the Tentmaker, He would surely know
Where one such rotting tent should go.
To have this canvas revitalized,
To have these poles and pegs resized,
To renew the rope that held it tall.
I'll see that Man, He knows it all.
Well, I went to Him on bended knees
Begging Him, "Tentmaker, please!
Restore this tent that I thought would last.
This canvas house that went so fast."
He looked at me through loving eyes
And merely pointed to the skies.
"Can't you see that mansion there?
It's built for you and I'm the stair.
So please don't grieve over some old tent.
Some canvas walls that have been spent.*

Marjorie M. Beyersdorf

*For this mansion that's been built by me
Will last you for eternity."*

After that, Robert's son shared what he had written entitled, "The Battle of My Gods".

The Battle of My Gods
By Evan Stanelle

[December 18, 1995]

*The sin was set a thousand year—
The encroachment of the serpent.
Death put to play in earthly hearts
By Eve and her companion.
Thus, the line of sin began—
Sprung from the tree of knowledge.
So close to death does life forego;
the line our piquant bondage.
From paradise does sin begin
And multiply heir hence,
To conductive properties of the soul,
the cancer of death thrice pence.
Cain and Abel...City of Gomorrah;
Humanity far and near.
The disobedience of a God
Who demands respect and fear.
In accord doth sin so spread,
Infecting all that cry.
Because of sin perpetuate,
The Son was sent to die.
The ultimate in history
Were eternity ever to feel...
Crushing the temptuous serpent's head
Who could only strike his heel.
So enter the second covenant—
The coming of an age.
Forgiveness of the sins of man
And the return in which they stage.*

My Story: Faith, Family, Farm

Thus, eternal death is overcome,
But the temporal remains as potent.
The apple fallen to the ground
Plants seeds that multiply.
From earth was man begot such that
In Earth, the seeds have grown—
From generation to family since
eternity has ever known.
Accordingly the fallen seeds
Were bound to reach my father—
From soul to soul the infection spreads
With the time to heal a bother.
So the fallen chain of sin,
From parent to offspring,
Found its way to infect our past
And the future that it brings.
For me my past—my mother and my father—
Common victims to the fall,
Set the stage for death's sweet play
And the falseness of its call.
My mother lives to tell her stay,
So I will not contend,
But my father's stage and fallenness
Is coming to an end.
Therefore, I will recount for you
My perceptions of the one
Who angrily defied the Lord
And named me as his son.

By nature, humanity is poor
And my father was no exception.
The fallen apple reached his blood
The moment of his conception.
I don't doubt my father's rebuttal—
To make atonement for his sin—
The works, the law, the gracious call
From the Father who brings us in.
But somewhere within the knocking
And the answering of the Lord,
My father stopped to contemplate
The possibility of strength accord.
Thus, began the life we know—

Marjorie M. Beyersdorf

The popular, powerful portrait—
A man who did not fear a fear
And the love that comes before it.
For love cannot be experienced
Without fearing the one who loves;
And love cannot be shared outright
If love does not start from above.

Hence my father did not fear,
Thus, setting the stage for war...
Between a love that calls for fear
And the sin in which it bore.

One corner stood my father
And in the other stood the Lord;
Their magnificence clashed head to head,
Temporal strength on its own accord.
And as Lewis has said in 'Miracles'
To bring rise on its own accord
Means to separate from creation grown
And classified as Lord.
So my father battled God—
Disobedient obstinance—
And in his torrent unbeknownst
His seeds were thus dispensed.
But God did not let his seeds be planted near the weeds,
Rather, the Lord called them his own—
Waiting, protecting, nurturing them—
Not stopping till full grown.
So as my father slowly fell
To a power greater than he,
All the good he ever held
Was planted in his seeds.
And as the Lord slowly tore
The obstinance from my dad,
He let him know with each painful tear
The greatness of his hand.

I don't believe my father lost...
I think he finally surrendered;
An exchange of fear for holy love
And the beauty that it renders.

Therefore, my father's story ends
In peace with the accord,
Not on his strength or with his wit
But the greatness of the Lord.
I miss my father...I always have,
His loss will be my strength,
But in my closing and my thanks
Give heed to God's great strength:

The Lord shall not be captured,
Defended or subdued.
The Lord shall not be overcome,
Dismissed or misconstrued.
For our Lord is Christ the Tiger,
The core of love and fear.
Our Lord is the great "I AM"
And is found in every tear.
My father's death today
Is not the end of a long told story,
Rather, my father's death today
Is a work of God's great glory.
So take my father and his apple
And learn from his long war,
That fear and love are eminent
To understand the cross Christ bore.

When Robert came up by us, never did I realize what a journey we would be on together! I mentioned about how returning home after having attended the centennial observance of this very church, I had walked into Robert's bedroom and shouted, "Hey Robert, Mom's home!" His voice was taken from him so he couldn't talk, but he smiled from ear to ear.

After saying that, I looked directly at the casket and said, "Robert, I know you can't hear me now, but I know if you could, you'd say, "Hey Mom, I'm Home!"

Marjorie M. Beyersdorf
Another Time of Sorrow

Christmas that year wasn't the usual. The house wasn't trimmed, and there wasn't a Christmas tree. More than ever, I knew a "real" Christmas wasn't comprised of material things, but truly knowing God through Jesus and having His Spirit within amidst the sorrow, and experiencing joy and peace in Him.

On the heels of bereavement of our son came another time of sorrow. On January 16, 1996, Lanetta's fiancé, Tim, passed away. Lanetta and Tim had gone shopping with me a little over a month ago, where they helped pick out a dress for me to wear at my son's memorial service. Between the choice of two, Tim pointed to the one he liked and that was the one I picked.

It was on April 18th, a year ago, when Tim had surgery for brain cancer. It was successful, and Tim went back to work. In the late fall of 1995, Tim started to experience dizziness and have headaches. After going to Mayo Clinic, they found the cancer had returned and it was inoperable.

Rather than stay in the hospital, he returned home with Lanetta. She called me and said, "Tim's not doing so well; could you come?" I went and spent time with him, remembering how I'd encourage him to eat his meals and how we would laugh together. His days were short, and we were with him at the time of his passing on January 16th. It was sad to see Lanetta's fiancé die so young.

Lanetta was kept very busy in her restaurant. I spent some time with her, and remember helping her make "Shish kebobs for two" as a Valentine's Day special. She appreciated my help and our time spent together.

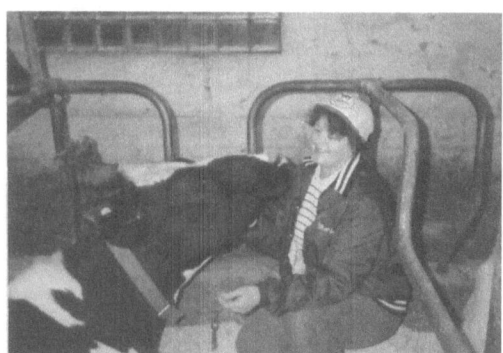

Marjorie with a Holstein cow, 1996

Marjorie, Runner-Up for the Wisconsin Farm Woman of the Year, 1996

My Story: Faith, Family, Farm

First Runner-Up

After returning home to the farm, extra time was required of me when I was encouraged to fill out forms to enter the competition for State Farm Woman of the Year. It used to be Farm Wife of the Year; then it was changed due to many women in agriculture being single or divorced.

In spring, I received recognition and a certificate for the completion of the Farm Business and Production Management course. It was presented at an evening banquet held at North Central Technical College. Plus, I had the honor of being the Master of Ceremonies!

A few days later, I received a letter in the mail, which stated I was chosen as one of three finalists in the state competition for Farm Woman of the Year. Wow! Coming home from the city of Wausau, in one of the street-side newspaper stands, I couldn't believe what I saw! My picture was dead center, on the front page of the local newspaper. I remember having a news reporter come to the farm and take pictures. I didn't ever expect I would make the front page as the cover girl! That was crazy!

A banquet was held in Colby, Wisconsin, and my whole family was invited as guests. We had a very special evening together. I was presented with a beautiful large plaque in the shape of the State of Wisconsin. On it was a golden cow, and engraved on it was "Farm Woman of the Year Runner-up".

With those activities passed, life settled down with the routine work and all on the farm. Until...our feed nutritionist came to the farm and said, "You'd make a good director on our local cooperative board." He placed my name on the nomination list. At the fall annual meeting, an election was held and I was voted in as the director. This meant commitment to monthly meetings, as well as special meetings that were held. It was quite an experience of contributing and learning in the operations and the pulse of agriculture.

Another harvest was completed as the cold weather was settling in. It was a time of special thanksgiving for all the crops, and years of blessings around a table of plenty. With turkey and all the trimmings, we had our favorite potato dumplings, garden veggies, and lots of good pies. So tasty!

I heard "White Christmas" sung by Bing Crosby on the radio, and such as it was, it was not a dream. There was snow on the ground! My thoughts turned toward Christmas, with all its preparations. I looked forward to being together with the whole family again. Now it was a countdown till the end of another year, and a welcome to 1997.

Marjorie M. Beyersdorf

***Jeremy, Marjorie, and Jeffrey Beyersdorf,
Most Improved Dairy Award, Double M Faith
Farm, 1997***

1997

Having been a student at North Central Technical College, it was brought to my attention that host families were needed for foreign exchange students. I had filled out an application the previous year, which resulted in having two boys live with us. One student, Ronald was from Honduras, and the other boy, Francisco was from Nicaragua. It was a learning experience to get to know their lifestyles and customs, as well as watching as they became acquainted with ours.

They were so amazed at the washing machines we had, as their lifestyles were much more rustic. They were used to dirt roads, no TV, no water faucets, things like that. Constantly expressing their appreciation to me, I would get frequent hugs and the days would end with "Goodnight Mum."

Having them was a huge commitment on my part. I had to take them to the bus stop every morning, and pick them up in the afternoon. Had they lived in the city, they'd be right there to get on the city bus. They became Green Bay Packer fans, as together we cheered the team on to victory while watching the Super Bowl game in our living room. It was a victory for sure, seeing the Packers become Super Bowl Champions on January 26th, 1997!

In February, Jeremy was seeing the dentist quite often. He had a protruding bottom jaw, which didn't allow him to bite and eat food normally. He had braces put on his teeth with the intent to have surgery in the near future. There were plans for the doctor to break his jaw in order to straighten it.

I recall going to Madison and appearing before our family insurance Board of Directors to plead with them about how Jeremy didn't have TMJ (insurance would not cover that). The dentist had sent the medical report along with me. Several days later, I received a letter informing us of their decision to cover the surgery expense. It was great news! Surgery was scheduled for 7:30 AM on July 7th.

With the fast passing of time, the day for surgery arrived quickly. Jeremy's mouth was wired shut when I saw him, and that night he stayed in the hospital. He had to drink through a straw; it was liquid nutrition for many weeks. It certainly wasn't easy for him, and it hurt me to see what he had to endure. Thankfully, Jeremy's friend, Roger, helped milk the cows in his place. Our hired hand and Jeff were busy chopping hay in the silo.

I was feeling the need for companionship, someone to enjoy things with and share good times together. So, through a friend of mine, I met a man through a referral service who had a farm near Marshfield. I went to visit his farm, and he likewise came to visit our farm. In mid-July, he asked me to go with him and his neighbors to the Farm Progress Days held near Manitowoc. We would be driving right past Lanetta's restaurant, so we stopped in to surprise her and say hi.

After I was caught up with all the garden work, and with the boys doing the farm work, I was free to go with my friend to visit his sister in South Dakota. On the way home, we stopped to visit his mother in Walnut Grove, Minnesota. We stayed overnight with her, and on the next day, we visited the *Little House on the Prairie* site where the original Ingalls Homestead was located. We walked along Plum Creek where Laura played many times along its banks. *Little House on the Prairie* was something we always watched as a family, so I really enjoyed seeing it all.

September found my friend and I visiting his mother and brother in Minnesota. His brother and family took us to see the Mall of America. The immensity of it all impressed me. I was also happy to tour Lakeland Veterinary Supplies in Eden, Minnesota, where we got our medical supplies for the farm. Their representative had visited our farm many times. What a fun trip!

Finally, the day Jeremy had patiently waited for had come. It was on October 23rd when he went to the dentist to remove his braces. I was so thankful! All turned out well, and his braving it out had resulted in a normal bite in his mouth.

Later that month, Lanetta held a Halloween costume party in the banquet hall of her restaurant. There were two people dressed up as cows, but nobody knew who they were. Upon revealing ourselves, it was quite a surprise! It was my friend and I. We had left his farm at 8:30 PM, arriving at the restaurant at 11:00 PM. We had so much fun at the party, and didn't leave there until 3:30 AM. We were back at his farm at 6:00 AM to milk the cows, and then I headed home. That's what you call living hours to the maximum! What an amazing night!

A couple living about four miles from home had asked if I would be interested in helping them out in their seasonal business, which consisted of making Christmas wreaths, swags, and evergreen roping. As if I needed more work! But I didn't mind. I agreed to help out. I'd go in the morning after milking at 8:00 AM and stay until 4:00 PM. My job was operating the sewing machine in the making of the evergreen ropes. Oh, how I enjoyed the aroma of the evergreen boughs!

I worked there twenty days in November and the first five days of December. The extra money was appreciated just in time for Christmas—like Christmas Club money—with which I bought gifts.

Jeremy took an off-farm job in Wausau at the Marathon Rubber Plant. He went in at 6:30 AM and worked till 3:00 PM. This curtailed his help in the barn in the mornings, but we managed.

December was full of transactions! We had purchased a used F150 Ford pickup truck. I signed the papers, registered it, and all complete; it was now ours!

There was a state law that underground fuel tanks needed to be dug out, and property could not be sold with them being underground. Toward the end of the month, a representative came to the house and explained to me how we could get this task accomplished. He had forms which I needed to fill out and sign. At the time, no date was set for when the removal of the tanks would be.

My dad's brother, Uncle Joe, and his wife, Mary Jane, who lived near Eagle River, Wisconsin called. He said they were coming to Wausau for some Christmas shopping and would like to take us out for dinner in the evening. We met at Michael's Restaurant, and after the meal, the boys wanted to make another stop. Uncle Joe said he'd take me home. As I sat in the back seat of their new 1996 Lincoln Town Car, with its leather seats and all the bells and whistles, I thought, Wow, I'd never dream I could own a car like this! Or could I?

For our Christmas Eve family time, we met at Lanetta's home for its observance and the exchange of gifts. Her living area was connected and all under the same roof with the restaurant. Plenty of food was available there!

Time seemed so short-lived when we were together. The boys left in the early morning for home to do the milking and chores. I stayed overnight for Christmas Day with Lanetta, then returned home. In just a few days, so closed another year.

1998

With winter settled in, and the barn chores and milking finished, we'd head into the house to enjoy its warmth and our off-work time. I was kept busy with bookwork, housework, and meals, plus evening meetings. There were more Co-op meetings now due to building a new C-store, and the studying of merger options with another cooperative.

I did have times off when I'd visit my friend. I'd go help him, and in return he would come to our farm and help us. One time, we went to see the movie *Titanic* together. The theater was so packed that we couldn't even sit together, and ended up on opposite sides of the room.

On February 27th, we started to milk three times a day again. That meant keeping up with the clock, every eight hours, milking cows. Thoughts also turned to spring and planting time. Our agronomist came to lay out plans for the new crop season, which fields needed to be soil tested, and what crops would be planted where, according to crop rotation.

Springtime again! Hearing the geese and seeing them fly overhead, as well as seeing the first robin, was always a thrill to me!

At the end of March, another couple, along with my friend and I, attended the All-Electric Farm Show in Green Bay, Wisconsin. There was a special show price on a wire welder, which I purchased for the farm shop. The boys went to the show two days later during the end of it, and picked up the welder. It would come in handy for farm repairs, and was a great addition to the shop.

A nearby farm of two hundred sixty-six acres, which had been rented for ten years, had a first option to purchase in the rental contract. I presented the option to purchase to the owners and they didn't want to sell it. So I contacted an attorney in Madison on April 3rd, and he came to our farm. Together we went to look at the property to be purchased. There was so much controversy over buying the farm! It came down to having us go to court at a later date. I had the legal right to exercise the first option to purchase, but the owners were surprised that I did!

On May 4th, which was a beautiful spring day, I was on my way to visit my Aunt Norma, who was my surrogate mother. She had moved into an apartment in Hilbert, a nearby village. Now Grandfather's house was vacant! After spending time with Aunt Norma, I left for Lanetta's and stayed overnight there. I helped her do some cleaning, then I left for home just in time to do the late evening milking.

The third weekend of May, my friend and I went to his niece's wedding in Walnut Grove, Minnesota. We stayed overnight with his mom in her home. While I was there, my grandsons came and helped Jeff and Jeremy on the farm, besides the boys' friends coming to help too. There was always someone over. It was very seldom when there was a meal with just the boys and I.

But lately, Jeff had been spending a lot of his time at his dad's place. Toward the end of May, he up and left and stayed with his dad. What a hurt that was to me! I was so thankful that neighbors helped us out in finishing the corn planting. Jeff had done most of the fieldwork. Now Jeremy chimed in to help. He handled the last planting of oats and peas. I never did the field work—my expertise was taking care of the cows.

With June came the cutting of hay. Jeremy cut and chopped the hay in the silo. A neighbor helped do most of the cutting with our Haybine. In fact, he had an accident while cutting it. Since the brake wasn't engaged as he stepped out of the Haybine, the hydrostatic machine drove right over him as it was turning in circles, fracturing his leg. We had to call an ambulance to take him to the hospital. I picked up his daughter and we followed the ambulance to the hospital, where I spent time with the family. Thankfully, he wasn't killed.

On June 7th, I received a phone call from my ex-husband about our daughter, Mary, telling me that she was in the hospital in Madison. Her diagnosis turned out to be Guillain-Barre Syndrome. The hospital did a procedure called plasmapheresis, which helped her.

Three days after the call, I had arranged to go visit. Lanetta was there also. After the visit, I went to Tom and Mary's farm, stayed overnight, and the next day, Mary's sister-in-law came and we cleaned the house. The kitchen got cleaned, floor and all. All the laundry was done up, too.

After three days there, I left for home. As I was arriving back in the afternoon, I found out that Jeremy had switched back to two-time milking. I couldn't blame him; it had gotten to be too much work. He was also kept busy working with the hay crop. Good thing the boys' friends were always helping out! And toward the end of the month, Jeff came back to the farm to help chop in the last of the hay.

Time came for our foreign exchange students to return to their countries. I gave them a farewell party on June 27th. That word that I really dislike—good-bye—came into play. Ronald and Francisco had lived with us for a year and a half, and had become a part of the family! I'm sure they would miss us, as we would miss them.

Barely a month later, we welcomed a German student, a young fellow named Willie into our home. I went to meet him at the airport on August 7th. He would be living with us as his "host family" for one year while attending North Central Technical College here in Wausau. My maternal grandparents had come from Germany and I looked forward to learning about another new culture.

Willie had the advantage of having a driver's license, so transportation from me wasn't needed for him to attend school. He was a studious boy and didn't engage in outside work.

Ah, but life is so daily! Always cleaning to do, if not in the house, it was in the barn too. Now we were getting the barn ready for the whitewasher to come. Everything was taken out of the barn—ropes, forks, pails etc. Two men came. First, they blew down dust and cobwebs with high-pressured blowers; and then, they used a mixture of lime ingredients and water with which to spray the walls and ceilings. When the barn walls dried, they were clean and white. And after the windows got washed inside and out, the barn looked great!

A Big Mistake

Guys and cars go together. Jeremy had always wanted to buy a classic car, and with my help, he purchased a Camaro. Jeff had a Duster. My grandson, Eric also had a classic car. He'd come to the farm with his car, and together they'd be washing and polishing them, or entering them in classic car shows through the summer and fall. They were all so proud of their cars!

With the growing season winding down, our apple trees were loaded with apples. It was on a cold October day that I met Khaek, Jeremy's girlfriend (who later became his bride). Khaek, Jeremy, and I shared time together picking all the apples from the trees.

A few weeks later, the boys built a cabin in our woods for deer hunting. At present, they were getting it ready for a bachelor party for my grandson, Evan. The cabin had a cook stove, bunk beds, table, and chairs. It even had a rigged-up shower and indoor toilet—rustic, but it fit the need.

One week later, Lanetta and Bob picked me up. We enjoyed the beautiful fall weather on the way as we drove to Evan's wedding in Eau Claire, where his bride, Christa, lived and where the ceremony would be held.

Jeremy approached me one day, saying he really didn't want to farm anymore. Not that he didn't like to work; it just wasn't what he wanted to spend his life doing. I did know his patience was short when it came to the cows. He was also gone often to Eau Claire, where Khaek was attending college.

I had been continuing my company with my friend throughout the past months, going to his farm to help him, and he in turn coming to help us when I needed it. Things seemed to always be happening, and "happen fast" they did!

The boys thought it would be a good idea to take the cows and young stock to my friend's farm. They were realizing just how much work the farm and its responsibilities had become for me, and he had a lot of feed and a very big barn, but not really a large milking stall area. Talk was tossed around, and I thought for sure my friend would be accommodating! I found out soon enough that wasn't the case.

Before I realized what was really happening, on November 14th, 1998, the heifers were in a truck heading for a farm near Marshfield. The following weekend, deer hunting season began. My ex-brother-in-law and the boys would be hunting. They would spend time in the cabin in our woods, staying there overnight. I usually did all the milking of the cows alone.

Thanksgiving week came and I had extra baking, turkey, and trimmings all to get ready. Two days before Thanksgiving, ten more cows left for the Marshfield farm. All the while I was wondering: what is really happening? I felt like driftwood going down the river, driven by a fast current! Then, two days after Thanksgiving, I hauled our little calves down there in our own small cattle trailer. Having all the young stock at the farm near Marshfield, the cows would go next.

On the evening of December 3rd, Lanetta came up and the boys and I ate together at Ponderosa. December 4th was the start of a weekend that was never to be forgotten! All my cows were going for a ride to a new home.

I rode with Lanetta; she had boxes of my clothes in her car. After she left, my friend and I started milking. It was nine o'clock in the evening. There were only forty milking stalls and cows had to be switched in and out of stalls several times. It took us four hours to milk, finishing up at one o'clock in the morning. Can you imagine doing that twice a day?!

Here we go again! Six o'clock in the morning, milking was started and we finished at noon. *Yes, noon!* Six hours of cows being in a new location, being chased back and forth; what a mess!

I noticed the cows started to bellow a lot; however, being in a new place, I didn't take it seriously—they'd get over it—until I discovered they weren't getting any water. This started on Saturday afternoon. We had to do something! We couldn't drill a new well that quickly, so I suggested we get a fire truck with water in temporarily and get someone to come and check the water pump. But my friend didn't act upon anything! That evening after work, I slept only three hours, being very stressed out.

The morning came really fast. On Sunday morning, we milked cows from six o'clock till ten-thirty. Still no water! Cows were crying. What a muddled mess.

Never, never will I forget that day. I had gone into the kitchen crying and praying to God. *This cannot go on!* Had I prayed before all this, in making decisions? No! I confessed I had made a big mistake.

I received peace in my heart and I knew what I had to do; undo the wrong. Rapidly, I reached for the telephone and called the trucker. His answer was yes; he'd contact the other drivers and come haul the cows back to their real home. In his remarks, he asked me if I was sure I wanted to do this. "Yes," I said, "Please come."

It didn't take long before seven trucks came, each one backing up to the barn and loading up the cows. My friend was in shock, never expecting me to do that. We had a caravan of cows coming back to their original home! I called the boys. Actually, they had thought it was a great idea that the cows would leave so they wouldn't have any more work with them. Were they ever surprised! I followed the trucks with my car, crying, singing and praying. *"Thank you, thank you, Lord. We're going home!"*

The following day, we went with one trucker to get the heifers, but my friend didn't let us take them. I did go in the house and took all the things of mine that I had put there. Two days later, we went back to get the young stock. With me were all their vaccination slips, and we checked them off one by one as they loaded the truck. The police were there to make sure there were no hassles.

All the cows came back home, except two little heifer calves. One was born there and one did not have a tag on it. My friend wouldn't let them go, claiming they were his. Jeremy said, "Leave them here; they'll be hostages."

The veterinarian was called out the following week for a couple cows that were sick. I told him what all had transpired and he laughed. "Some gals take their dogs or cats for a weekend; you took your cows!"

"Yes," I said, and we both laughed. But it certainly wasn't a laughing matter at the time! Thankfully the cows recovered and I was back home milking cows alone.

Christmastime arrived, with all the preparations needing to be done. With the boys' help, we did milking earlier than usual. Then it was off to Lanetta's for Christmas Eve. Jeff drove down separately. Jeremy and I went together, leaving at seven o'clock and arriving back home at four o'clock in the morning after sleeping a couple hours before traveling.

Jeremy had started to work at Kolbe & Kolbe here in Wausau, and on December 29th, he moved out and into his dad's place. It seemed both boys needed their time with him.

Chain of Reactions

A New Year came, 1999, and it was a "chain of reactions" with one action leading to another. It was a very cold winter and the final year of another decade.

As winter usually does, it often creates more work due to the cold and snow. There was one day all the drinking cups froze up. I had hired a fellow to help with the farm work, as it was getting hard to do a lot of it alone. Lanetta and I talked about getting rid of the cows. She told me a cattle dealer where she lived would be interested to come up and look at the herd.

In the beginning of January, Lanetta came along with the dealer and one other person, but things didn't pan out. At times, I entertained the thought of having an auction of all the equipment and cows, and renting out the land. Not knowing anything about auctions, I called an auctioneer and made an appointment on February 13th to get more information. I didn't have him out to the farm to schedule the auction, but with his slick talking, we were scheduling an auction for March 4th.

The next day was Sunday and I was in church. I don't know how to describe it, but I had no peace at all about what took place the day before. I knew in my heart it wasn't the right decision to make. On Monday morning I called the sales office, and told them to cancel the auction.

The auctioneer had already put a listing out in the newspaper. One of my cousins sent me the clipping as it appeared in the paper. It had a large "X" across it, saying it was cancelled. To me, it was like seeing an obituary of the farm, but thankfully "X'd" out!

I had an appraisal of the farm equipment done to get an estimate of what all the machinery would be worth. Jeff, at this time, had started working at a repair shop where they were doing tractor overhauls. It was about an hour's drive for him to go to work. "These cows suck," I remember him saying after coming home from work. I had to tell him the silo unloader wasn't working, which meant he had to climb up the silo and see what the problem was. Work on the farm never ended.

On March 6th, I received news that Aunt Norma had died. I was sad to hear that; she had been my surrogate mother for many years. I left the evening before the funeral, and stayed with Lanetta overnight. At events such as this, all the relatives came together for a short time of visiting and seeing each other again.

I was thankful that Jeremy came to help on the farm while I was gone. "Inevitable" is one true description of life! My own life was never at a standstill.

Time Clock Punching Begins

In mid-March, a prominent dairy man, Gary Van Der Geest, came to the house. We talked at great length about his interest in buying my herd of cows, and him wanting me to come work for him at his farm. He shared with me his plans of building a larger milking parlor with more cows, and how he would need more employees. My answer at the time was, "I will get back in touch with you."

I went to see my loan officer to discuss financial matters regarding the cows being sold and having the cropland rented out to the same party. All seemed to be working toward that direction. It was a good time of discussion with my son, Richard, when he took me out to eat on my birthday, March 27th. We talked about me farming alone versus selling the herd of cows, and about me going to work where my cows were going. I decided I'd go with them!

Four days later, trucks backed up to the barn door, the milk cows were loaded, and I watched as they headed out to their new home. Lanetta came up for the day to support me, thinking it would be hard for me to see the cows go. In the evening, Jeff, Jeremy, Lanetta, and I went out to eat. I exclaimed, "No milking cows here, now or in the morning!"

On April 1st, the cattle trucks came to haul the dry cows and all the heifers with calves in them. Without the cows to milk, and only a few heifers left yet to be picked up, I took the opportunity to visit with Mary. We enjoyed cleaning together, looking for mushrooms in the woods, and going out for pizza. After spending three days with her for a short vacation, there was the need to return home and help load the last of the cows off our farm.

April 14th was a red-letter day in my life. I was punching a time clock for my first day of work. It was just two weeks earlier when the cows went to their new farm. The cows went, and yes, I followed after them!

My work there was in the medical barn, monitoring the pregnant cows. When they were ready to have their calves, I would bring them into the birthing pens and assist if needed during the births. Feeding the baby calf its first milk (colostrum), tagging it, and charting the cow and calf numbers were all enjoyable tasks for me. Then, it was up into the calf barn—the nursery—and on to the next one. Helping to milk the fresh cows and the medicinal-treated cows was also part of my work.

Being taught how to IV a cow wasn't easy. I hadn't done it before; it was hard for me to thread the needle back so it was seated directly in the vein. As my confidence grew, I'd say to myself, "You can do it" and I did!

The work hours were long; many times, sixteen to seventeen hours a day, six days a week. I started at four o'clock in the morning and worked till eight or nine at night.

New herds of cows were purchased by my employer. Another person, along with me, would milk them. Having new cows in a different environment was always a challenge in milking them. We wouldn't know which side they were used to being milked on, and so we were always on guard, wary about getting kicked or slammed from one side of the stall to the other.

After several months, my start time was changed to come in at midnight; the reason being was that no one was around in the barn after the evening parlor cows were milked. The workers would be finished around eleven o'clock. Any calves being born after eleven had nobody to take care of them. That's when I primarily started to be "in charge" of the birthing area.

When I had time off from my job, I kept busy in spring and summer by taking care of the lawn work, and the flowers I liked to plant. I had a garden, which was cut down in size, so it didn't take a whole lot of time.

Then, there were always the extra challenges that presented themselves. There had been a deposition with my attorney from Madison and myself, along with the farm owner and his attorney, regarding the purchase of the land I was renting. I had presented a "first option to purchase" to the owner, and they didn't want to sell. The option was a written agreement in the rental contract made out by his attorney.

The month of August started with a new experience; me on the witness stand in court for three days. There was a six-person jury, and I thought, All this just to purchase land! On the third day, the verdict was given that I would be able to purchase the property. The jury had sided with us, and all the court costs would be paid for by the opposing party.

I'll never forget the experience of sitting in the courtroom alone, while the others had gone out, as I waited for the jury's decision. The solemn environment elevated my thoughts to the time when I would be before

God in His Presence, where true justice would be meted out. I prayed a prayer of thankfulness to God for His Son, Jesus, because I knew I would someday come before God in the righteousness of Jesus, who is my Savior. He paid the penalty for my sins, the penalty for which I so rightly deserved to pay.

My Son Becomes the Farmer

Meanwhile, Jeff had discontinued his work at the tractor repair shop. The distance of driving back and forth was too much, so he considered working at the big farm where I worked. He came and talked to my employer about working there, and two days later he started. His job was operating a huge tractor up on top of the silage bunkers, packing down the silage. He also drove the feed trucks. It was a short sprint of work for Jeff. Punching a clock wasn't his style!

Unbeknownst to me, Jeff wanted to get a herd of cows for himself and milk on our farm. When he finally confided in me, I cried when I heard all this. I had sold the new milk machines I had, the vacuum pump, chopper boxes, and two big fans out of the barn. Had I known his desire to farm, these items would not have been sold.

An agricultural instructor from North Central Technical College came to our home to go over a financial plan with Jeff. He also alerted him about a good dairyman, which he had heard about, who was interested in selling his cows. Jeff asked me to go along with him to look at the cows, the farm not being too far out of our area. The cows looked great; they were mapped, with excellent genetics. Buying a closed herd was the way to go; not buying cows from all different places.

That same evening, I received a phone call from Uncle Joe Lingle asking if I'd like to have their Mercury Marquis station wagon. Five days later, Jeremy and Khaek took me to Conover, not far from Eagle River, where they lived. I had answered "yes" to Uncle Joe's question, and now I was on my way home in my station wagon. He thought we could haul feed sacks, but I said, "Oh no, Uncle Joe, it's too good for that!"

On November 1st, the property we had rented was now my own. Signing the papers, along with all the transactions, took place at People's State Bank in Wausau. *What a welcomed day!* To know that now, after a couple of years of trying to purchase farmland, it was all finalized!

As I mentioned the beginning of this year, 1999, it was "a chain of reactions" with one action leading into another. Well, on November 3rd, forty cows moved into our barn, along with six heifers. I was happy to see it all happen. The barn wouldn't stand empty over winter, and Jeff was now a farmer!

At work, there were new employees hired from South Africa—a family consisting of a dad, mom and two children. They moved into the small house on the farm there, and we enjoyed working together in the medical barn. I had made the traditional Thanksgiving dinner, and invited them over to share the meal with us. It was a good time of learning about each other's families.

Every year, I'd write a Christmas letter rather than send Christmas cards to my relatives and friends. But it was one thing after another! I finally started writing the letter a week before Christmas.

On Christmas Eve, Jeremy, Khaek, and I drove to Lanetta's in the early evening. Jeff came after milking the cows. It was so nice having our family together, enjoying the exchanging of gifts, and remembering the "Greatest Gift" ever; a Baby born in a manger over two thousand years ago, "...and His Name shall be called Jesus, for He shall save His people from their sins" (Matthew 1:21).

A New Decade Begins

A new decade, wow! The year was 2000. Years ago, when we'd look ahead, 2000 seemed far out in the future, and now here it was!

This year was much quieter than the past couple of years. Life seemed to be more settled down. I continued my work at the large dairy farm, and Jeff was farming at home. The cropland was his now, to crop for his cattle needs. Last year, I had it rented out to my employer; this year, Jeff was the renter.

It was great to welcome the warmer weather of spring! I'd be outside, raking the lawn and preparing the flower beds. The time soon came to mow all the grass. I didn't look at all this as work, because I really enjoyed it—a hobby is what I called it!

My ex brother-in-law, who lived in Neenah, would come up to help Jeff at different times. Plus, a couple of Jeff's friends helped with the field work. Oft times, I'd milk his cows so they could finish the field work they were doing.

Summer went by like a flash! Corn silage was being chopped in the silo, and the custom combining people came to combine the corn for high-moisture, to be put into the Harvestor.

I took off from work for several days at the end of October to go down and visit Mary. It was always good to spend time working together.

On October 28th, we went to Richland Center, to Mary's hairdresser, and I got my hair trimmed and set. We ate the noon meal together where my granddaughter, Shannon, was working. Afterwards, I headed for Wausau, only to be home about an hour before I left to attend Jeremy and Khaek's wedding ceremony at five o'clock. It was a very full and eventful day!

On the evening of November 1st, I had gone to work, and before getting to the punch clock, one of the workers met me. He informed me that our employer, Gary, had a fatal heart attack in his office a few hours before I arrived.

My work hours had always gone like clockwork in the morning, with Gary coming into the medical barn at 5:00 AM. You could set your watch by him! He and I would get the fresh cows into their milk stalls so they were ready to be milked when the workers came in. On November 2nd, I realized he would not be there at five o'clock. I would never again hear him say, "Good morning, Marge!" with his big smile, cowboy hat, and colorful shirts that he always wore. I had an empty feeling in my heart for a while. He was truly missed.

Gary had hired me a year and a half ago. I was thankful to have been able to work for him, and appreciated what he taught me regarding cows. I remember him saying to me once, "Take care of my cows, as if they were your own. I know you will."

And yes, I did!

Jeff and I went to the wake at the funeral home and stood in line for over one and a half hours to view the casket. So many people had come to pay their respects. The following day I attended the memorial service at his church, which was attended by a large crowd.

At the November cooperative meeting, our annual meeting for the stockholders, I was re-elected as a director on the board. This meant the "monthly night out" meetings didn't stop!

The weeks slipped by and already it was family time on Thanksgiving Day! Lanetta, her boyfriend John, Bob, Richard, Jeff, and I all enjoyed our turkey and potato dumplings, and all that went with it. This year, Jeremy and Khaek had gone to her relatives in Virginia for Thanksgiving, and Mary wasn't able to come home.

Next came all the Christmas preparations in the month of December, and continuing work at the big farm. Time went by so fast; before I knew it, Christmas Day was here, and soon after, the close of another year!

Bob and I had stayed friends through the years, and together we helped

Mary celebrate her special day on January 7th. Our meeting place was in Stevens Point, after which Bob and I drove together to meet Mary for her birthday.

A week later, while I was at work, I was informed by my employer that Jeremy was at the hospital with a ruptured appendix. He had been taken to the ER, where, at four o'clock in the morning, an appendectomy was performed. Thankfully it had all turned out well!

Several co-op board meetings were held during the months of January and February. Being a director on the Cooperatives Board meant many late-night meetings.

Winter gave way to the arrival of spring, with the usual work: cleaning up the yards, planting time and lawn to cut. Then came the hot days of summer with hay harvesting, and later the fall corn harvest, with myself busy with our garden and the routine barn work with the cows. It seemed a flash in time as the year ended!

Action in 2002

Wow, it was two years already into the new decade! The beginning of 2002 started out with medical appointments for me; my annual physical check-up with my family doctor and my dentist, for dental work that needed to be done.

I had tax work; getting the records together from the previous year. Every month's business was computerized at Farm Credit, which simplified it a lot. In March, my new contact lenses were in at the eye doctor. I'd worn contacts since 1973.

March was birthday time for Lanetta and me, and in the coming month was Jeff's. Birthday celebrations were something we just couldn't stop having! And now spring was here, with the excitement again of seeing the first robins back, welcoming the warmer weather, and the soon-to-be time of the planting season.

A special evening in May had me on my way to Mary and Tom's farm for a graduation celebration for my grandson, Dwayne. I attended the evening commencement ceremony at the high school. The following day, Mary and Tom hosted a party for relatives and friends that was held at their farm. And so, each month brought its own happenings, besides all the routine work, and my outside employment.

Auctions were always exciting to go to, where the highest bidder gets to buy. Jeff asked me to go with him to a cattle auction where he bought eleven cows, and took them home with him. It was a successful trip in building his herd.

Clean-up in the barn began with the sweeping of cobwebs and washing the milk pipelines. Next, we washed the barn windows; with the last project being the tidying up of the milk house.

On June 25th, we had a tour from the YMCA daycare preschoolers, with their adults in charge. Excitement was displayed on each of the children's faces when they saw the baby calves, the cows, kittens, and our farm dog. For most of these little ones, it was their first experience of being on a farm, and seeing where the milk they drink comes from.

Each month brought with it different experiences. I was interested in buying a computer and had ordered a Gateway, which came on July 10th. After getting it all set up, now I had the challenge of learning how to use it. Years ago, we didn't have computers in school. Now, they were in all the classrooms. Business couldn't thrive without them.

With the hot and humid days of July upon us, it was family reunion time. This year it was hosted by my uncle, who lived in Fond du Lac, Wisconsin. It was held in one of the city parks there, and I enjoyed visiting together with all the relatives.

August was the start of a new project in the barn. Jeff tore out the old comfort stalls on the west side and new stalls were cemented in, along with rubber mats and new tiles in the manger. My ex brother-in-law came up to help, and Jeremy, too. Lanetta was there to help, also, on the day the tiles were cemented in. Many hands make light work! By the second week of September, the west side of the barn was completed. It was ready for the cows to enjoy, each to their own stall.

In October, I received a call from Uncle Joe. He and Aunt Mary Jane were moving to Kenosha, where they could be closer to their daughters. They had decided to get rid of their Lincoln town car. Uncle Joe remembered when we were up by them getting the Mercury Marquis, and what I had said to him. "I'll take this one, too." He'd said, "Nope! That one you can't have!"

Having made that comment then, he was calling to see if I was still interested in getting it. The dealers wouldn't give him what it was really worth, and before giving it away to them, he'd rather see me get it for a nominal price. So, the car that I sat in the back seat when we were taken out to eat with Uncle Joe and Aunt Mary Jane four years ago would now become mine! What an unexpected surprise! In the later part of October, Jeff took me up to get the car. Never would I have ever thought I'd own a '96 Lincoln town car!

A few weeks later on was Thanksgiving Day; not only was it a feast with turkey and all the trimmings, it was a special time of thanks for the daily provisions of life. As our family gathered around the table, we were truly thankful for God's care through another year; and His provision of a good harvest meant the cattle mangers wouldn't go empty.

Christmas time came with all its festivities, and soon after, we stood at the threshold of another new year.

2003: Of Donkeys and Family

The year 2003 was here! There is always that "something special" about a new year that brings a fresh start, with people making resolutions and plans, and setting goals for the coming year.

Dairy farming can have goals for the year, but it does have its same basic every day goals, too: feeding cows, milking cows, and cleaning out the barn behind the cows. There is spring crop planting time, hay-making time, grain harvest time, and all the "in betweens" that need to be done. Even though I wasn't farming myself at home, I still enjoyed the work and helping my son, Jeff.

In April, I took off four days from employment at the big farm to do chores and milking for Jeff, while he had a hernia surgery on April 12th. In between the chores, I did spring cleaning in the milk house. Inspection was due soon, and it would need to be "spic and span" clean when the inspector came!

At the end of April, I spent a day with our student, Damion. He was from Jamaica and had lived with us for a year in 2001 while he was attending North Central Technical College. The students arranged a pig roast in the park for their host families. What a great time we all had together, with many different countries represented by the students!

Lanetta came up in May to visit, and to get our heads together as we planned the family reunion for this year. Our family, my brother and I, and our children had charge of all the arrangements. We made advance notices to save the date, got them all ready, and mailed them out. The date was the last Sunday in July.

We planted a garden again, oh yes! That's my relaxation time! I enjoyed sitting and pulling weeds out by the roots (as they won't come back again that way). Then later came the picking of the produce and enjoying the good eating.

I planted and kept the flower beds especially nice with the lawns trimmed up, as the family reunion was being hosted at our farm. There was some extra cleaning in addition to the general house cleaning that had to be done. The basement especially needed it desperately!

A month went by fast, and here it was June already! Lanetta came up again so we could make the invitations for the family reunion. By the end of the day, they were addressed, stamped, and ready to be mailed out.

On July 17th, we bought two donkeys, the start of our donkey saga. At present writing, there are three jennies (females) and one jack (male). It was nice to have them before the family reunion for the extra amusement!

July 27th arrived, the day we hosted our family reunion! About fifty people came to enjoy the noon meal, which we catered in—broasted chicken, ham, coleslaw, and rolls. Salads and desserts were made by our family. The weather was good, and it was a beautiful day to eat outside.

Most everyone enjoyed a tour of the large dairy farm in the afternoon where I worked, eight miles west of our farm. The opportunity to see 3000 cows at one time, in a free stall barn one third of a mile long, isn't an ordinary experience; and to watch one hundred cows being milked all at one time. Wow!

Later in the afternoon, yes, there was more food again: ice cream, desserts, with the leftovers from noon. What a memorable day!

September brought a not so happy day when Jeff and I went to Jeremy and Khaek's house in Wausau to get some things and food they wanted us to take. They were finishing up their packing for their move to Virginia. With tears in my eyes, I said good-bye, and we left to go back to the farm. I knew we'd stay in touch, but I realized this meant we wouldn't be seeing them very often.

In the past years, I had dated several different fellows. My boys would say, "Mom, you could write a book on that alone!" We'd go out to eat, go to a movie, or just stay at home watching a video. I especially kept quite a close relationship with a fellow from Marshfield. It all seemed so right at the time. (However, God knew different! Like the time I took my cows for a weekend to Marshfield!)

The day came when I took all the letters I had received from different fellows over the years out to the gravel driveway, and lit a match to them. My thoughts went way back, to God's chosen people, the Israelites; how He had delivered them out of bondage in Egypt. Miraculously, they had escaped the enemy by crossing through the Red Sea on dry land! God cared for their daily needs, yet, they turned from Him in disobedience, never being satisfied. Because of their waywardness, God made them to wander in the wilderness for forty years.

Forty years, ah, Lord! I accepted You as my personal Savior in 1963, and now it was 2003. I knew You as my Savior, but not necessarily the

Lord of my life. Truly, I had spent over forty years "in the wilderness." I knew I was forgiven and delivered from all my sin and guilt, but I didn't necessarily give up my right to myself.

Every time I see a yield sign on the highway, it's a reminder that I must obey what it says and yield. Just as I obey that sign, I must surrender to Jesus Christ, yielding my life in all ways to Him as Lord. He is my Shepherd, my Lord and my Coming King.

It was Christmas time again, and I so enjoyed it! The time we celebrate when God revealed Himself in Jesus, born in flesh as you and I, yet perfect without sin. He was the God-Man! He was born to save people from their sins. It grips me more and more with each passing day; such wonderful, unconditional love, His Mercy and Grace, and all the Promises in His Word. I praise God for it all!

2004

Time came to welcome in the New Year, 2004! It was the fourth full year of Jeff's farming career, with myself continuing to work at the large dairy farm. Life continued to always be ongoing! Highlights of the year continued to happen, one of which was when Richard and his wife, Patti, took me with them to visit Aunt Letty, who was to be eighty years old. Aunt Letty lived in Savanna, Illinois, and we drove down on Saturday, May 8th, and stayed overnight in a motel. On Sunday, we had a surprise birthday party for her, and was she ever surprised!

Then in June, it was graduation time for my granddaughter, Shannon Lurvey. I was there in attendance at her commencement program on Friday evening, June 4th, and stayed overnight with the family. The following day, friends and relatives gathered at Mary and Tom's farm for a graduation party.

Life was one event after another! In July, on the 23rd, my granddaughter, Aimee Stanelle (Robert Jr.'s daughter) married Mike Hamilton. The wedding was held in Appleton. I always felt it was a great honor to be invited to a wedding, and what a beautiful wedding they had!

When the last Sunday in July came, it was family reunion time for my mom's side of the relation! That is one time for sure in the year we get to see each other. Not only one reunion this year, but another! The last Saturday of July was a large family reunion of my divorced husband's side of the relation. It was held at a park in Seymour. Yes, I attended; even though I was "X'd" out, I still kept in touch with cousins and aunts and uncles.

The middle of summer, attention was focused at home! A large project was starting on our house. A roofing and siding company came in and put new roofing on the house first, then all new windows, except the living room and kitchen window, which had been put in new several years ago.

After the windows, came new vinyl siding. At the family reunion at our place last year, one of my uncles said, "You'll have to look at doing something with the house pretty soon." And he was right! The exterior's wooden siding was chipping bad in many places. The roof leaked, and so did some windows when wind would sweep the rain in!

When the house was completed, I was so happy to tell my uncle about the new wheat-colored siding, accented with burgundy-colored shutters alongside the new windows. I said to him, "It doesn't look any more like it did when you were here." It was a much-needed project accomplished!

With corn harvest in full swing, for me, getting the garden cleaned up meant the colder days would soon be coming. Co-op Board meetings, church, Bible study, helping Jeff, my job, and housework made up my days, as another year was drawing to a close.

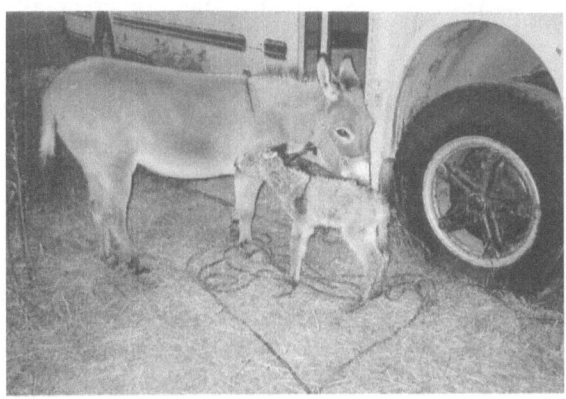

Jenny donkey and her baby

Marjorie M. Beyersdorf

Jenny

In 2005, I put a brand-new calendar on the wall, and already, the first month was filled with the usual appointments. There were dental appointments, an annual physical check with my doctor, and then came tax time, with its appointment. There were extra cooperative meetings, four alone in March, besides all the routine work. No time to slouch!

Planting season came, with all its usual work and the crops in the field, and for me, the garden work, flower planting and keeping up the lawns and yard. All in all, it occupied the summer.

There was excitement on the farm! It seemed like waiting would never end, in regards to our female donkey. She was pregnant and time was getting close for her to have her baby. We'd check every day, but nothing!

On a particular day in late summer, August 23rd, I was feeding the baby calves when I realized I hadn't checked on the jenny for a while, so I decided to go and check on her. There she was—Mama and her baby!

I ran to the barn to tell Jeff to come outside. I didn't tell him why. He figured it was the jenny, with the possibility something was wrong. Was he ever surprised! It was what we were waiting for so long. It was a female, and she stared at us with her long ears up, standing erect, alongside of her mom. They sure are the cutest when they are just born!

A big project on the farm had begun at the end of August—the building of a 128' x 30' heifer barn. It was set back away from the dairy barn, on the northeast corner of the farm. A lot of action took place for the next two months, with trucks and large equipment in and out of the yard. Large cement trucks brought cement for the floor; then trucks brought in the trusses and other lumber. It was quite a project.

On September 15th, I had given a two-week notice to my employer that I would be leaving my job at the large dairy farm. Jeff and I had talked about my helping him out more. We also discussed the situation of him buying the home farm. He had invested in the barn stalls being remodeled, yet I owned the farm.

I talked with the other children, but none of them were interested in the farm. It would be wise to make the decision soon, so if I'd be taken, the home farm of 171 acres, with all the buildings, would be his. There was another acreage of farmland which was formerly rented to another farmer, then purchased by me five years ago. Jeff continued to operate that with crop planting.

On September 22nd, with the move of the pen as I signed the real estate papers, ownership of the home farm was given to my son, Jeff.

Exciting news had come on September 15th; Jeremy and Khaek became parents of a baby girl, Hannah. They now had two daughters; Kyla was born four years ago and now Hannah! Another grandchild added to the list of eight!

My last evening of work on my job at the large dairy farm was September 29th. No more working the whole night through! It would be good to be able to go to bed at night, rather than sleeping during the day.

On October 28th, the heifer building was totally finished. The heifers went into their new home the beginning of November, after having been in a homemade corral outside.

Jeremy came home for the opening weekend of deer hunting. He flew in from Virginia on Thursday, November 17th, and left again by plane on Sunday evening. It was good to see him again!

The Christmas season came, and lifted the spirits of us all. The whole family, minus Jeremy, Khaek, and their kids, got together on Christmas Eve at the farm. It was such a great time together with everyone there; and a night always to be remembered as my last family Christmas Eve on the farm.

Leaving the Farm

So many happenings in my life didn't happen because of long-range planning. After the farm had been bought by Jeff, living with him—and him having a girlfriend—made me feel uncomfortable. She moved in with him, and more problems seemed to surface.

In 2006, on January 22nd, at the start of a new year, Lanetta called me. She said, "Mom, I think you'll have to move off the farm." It was like someone had dropped a brick on my head! *Was I hearing that right?*

Lanetta and Jeff had been talking a lot on the phone, and she knew more of just what was going on. I expected in the future I would be moving, as Jeff would have his own life now. But the farm had been just sold to him less than four months ago, and even he had said at the time of the sale to me, "Mom, you can stay living here." We continued on as we always had. I did the herd health records and helped milk cows, but communication was slim.

In February, I went to Atlanta, Georgia to attend a weekend health seminar. It wasn't my first airplane ride, but I did it alone. Jeff took me to the airport and came to get me when I arrived back on Sunday evening. It was an enjoyable experience learning all about new health products.

March 15th was Lanetta's birthday. It was a two-fold trip to visit her on her special day, plus we went to the bridal shop for a dress fitting for me, as the mother-of-the-bride. Lanetta had October 28th set as her wedding date.

On April 11th, I filled out an application with a senior care group. I wasn't helping Jeff as much with his girlfriend there, and besides, I needed something to do for an income. I was called in for my first day of work on April 21st. The client I worked with was a blind lady in Wausau, and we hit it off right away.

The tension at Jeff's was rising, so after church services on Sunday mornings, I would go and check out the houses for sale. My desire was not to rent, but to own a smaller home. One Sunday, a couple from church wanted me to have lunch with them. I told them there were a few open houses I wanted to go see. They said, "Good! We'd like to go with you, and see different homes, too."

They told me about a couple in church who had just listed their home for sale. "Really!" I said, and two days later, I was over to see them and their home. I liked their house very much. It was set back quite aways from the sidewalk, with not a large yard to keep up.

Help-U-Sell was my next stop. I told them I had looked at the house and was very much interested in purchasing it. I put money down on it so they would hold it for me.

Talk about moving fast! On April 27th, there was an inspection of the house, all papers were signed, and the insurance taken care of, which was followed with the closing on Friday, May 12th. That same evening, I went over to my new home and started cleaning the kitchen cupboards. The following day, Mary and her daughter, Sierra, came up to help pack my things. They stayed overnight with me on my last night on the farm that I loved so well!

On Sunday morning, my son Richard, Bob, and Lanetta came and helped me move. For the larger items, we made three trips with a small, rented U-haul truck. Mary and Sierra left on Sunday evening, but Lanetta stayed with me for my first evening in the city. This was a new experience for me, being a "country gal" living in the city!

Seniors and Cows

In April, there was one client I worked with for Home Instead. But by now, I was assigned two more folks to take care of. I enjoyed working with the older people. They were so happy to have me come by and see them! For some, I'd do their laundry, others I'd clean their floors, make meals, or take them grocery shopping. It was a variety of different tasks that I helped them with at their homes.

The beginning of June, I went down to visit Mary and Tom for my granddaughter Shianne's high school graduation. The commencement program was held on Friday evening, June 2nd. A month later, they hosted a graduation party for her on their farm for friends and relatives. It was a fun event, and Shianne was happy to be finished with high school and on to the next adventure!

On Saturday the 16th of September, I attended my grandson Eric's wedding in Madison. It was always good to be together with the family at happy occasions such as this.

Then the big day came for Lanetta's wedding on October 28th. I drove down to her place the day before the wedding. My brother, Richard and his friend, Mary came from Arizona. They stayed with me for a couple days afterwards, and it was so nice to visit with them.

In November, it was my first Thanksgiving turkey dinner prepared in my new home. My grandson Evan, Christa, and his family, Richard, and Bob all came for Thanksgiving Day. We were missing a few: Lanetta had to work, Mary and Jeremy couldn't come but called, and Jeff went by his girlfriend's grandma's place for dinner.

A turn of events happened later that month when I received an e-mail asking if I could come back to work at the big farm. The employer knew I wasn't working on Jeff's farm any more, since I had talked to him earlier in the year. So on December 1st, I went in to sign employment papers, and started work there on December 2nd. My shift was noon to midnight, twelve hours.

My main responsibility there was to monitor the pens of cows that would soon be giving birth. We had to walk amongst them every hour to check for signs of delivery, and then bring them into the birthing pens. I'd palpate the cow to see if the calf was positioned correctly, and to find out how she was dilating. We assisted in delivery only if it was needed. I would help treat the cows by giving shots and IVs. A thousand times over, I witnessed the miracle of life!

Meanwhile, I still had some morning clients with Home Instead. The blind woman I took care of lived en route to the big farm. I'd put my clean farm uniform on, and went from finishing work for her to the farm. Of course, she didn't know what I was wearing!

In between all my work, I was making preparations for Christmas, writing out my annual Christmas letter, decorating some, along with the cookie and strudel baking. I was thankful to have a daughter—Lanetta—

who liked to shop and did all the Christmas shopping for me. I do not like to go shopping!

Christmas Eve was held at Lanetta and John's home. All the family came together. I stayed overnight with them, and on Christmas Day, returned home for work at noon.

And so ended another year of the likes and happenings of which I'd never thought would be happening! Living in the city now, back working at the big farm, along with several senior folks I helped care for in the mornings. Such a busy year!

Marjorie with her children - Mary, Jeremy, Lanetta, Jeffrey, and Richard, 2007

2007

Recognizing birthdays has always been an important event in our family. Even after I left my first family, if at all possible, I'd spend time with each one of my children on their birthday. So it was on Sunday, January 7th that I met Bob at Target in Stevens Point, and we drove together to Bear Valley to Mary and Tom's farm for Mary's birthday. We had noon lunch and birthday cake together, leaving again for home in the late afternoon. I had baked the cake, and we brought along the chicken and sides to eat. It was a birthday treat for her!

My Story: Faith, Family, Farm

On March 21st, my doctor appointment revealed that I had a hernia on my left side. It would ache and it seemed there was a little bulge there; my supposition was right. I made arrangements to have surgery, scheduled at eight-thirty in the morning on March 27th. A hernia surgery! What an unusual birthday present for me on my birthday.

Lanetta came up to take me to the hospital, and after surgery she brought me back home, all in five hours. There was no going to work for the rest of the week.

On Easter Sunday on April 8th, after attending church service, Richard, his wife Patti, Bob, and I went out to eat for a special Easter dinner.

The following weekend, I went down by Mary. We did cleaning together, and I baked their favorite sweet rolls, some fruit pies and a torte for the family. Leaving there late Sunday evening brought me home just slightly before midnight.

Jeff's birthday on April 23rd had me stopping by the farm on my way to work. His favorite dessert is banana crème pie, so that is what I made for him in place of a birthday cake.

A highlighted day in May was Mother's Day. The family came up and we all ate out at King Buffet restaurant. The following Saturday, May 19th, we were together again. I met Bob, Richard, and Patti at Stevens Point, and then drove with them to attend granddaughter Shannon's high school graduation party at Mary and Tom's farm near Bear Valley.

The last Sunday in June was a fun day, also, when I attended "Sundae on the Farm" in Calumet County. Lanetta was on the dairy promotion committee. She spearheaded all the arrangements by ordering food, etc. for the event. It was a great day for not only farmers to get together to visit, but for city people to come to as well. There was all you can drink free chocolate and white milk, and free cheese, too. A great dairy day for all!

On July 3rd, the co-op board had a tour of all our feed mill facilities. I worked the whole week, and did take off for the co-op meeting, as we directors were making decisions for long-range planning and current facility needs.

Among the busy days came sad news. On July 14th, I answered my phone and learned my Uncle Harry Jr., one of my mom's brothers, had died. The funeral service was held on July 19th in Fond du Lac. I drove to Lanetta's, and then we drove together to attend the memorial service. Memories flooded back of my time as a child on Grandfather's farm and how Harry took me on his bike for a ride. I got my ankle caught in his bike spokes once and a scar remains today.

The first weekend of August was the total Stanelle family reunion at the Stanelle Homestead, the house where my brother and I were raised by Grandfather. Hundreds of invites were sent out. On Saturday evening, in a

107

rented hall, there was a sit-down, family-style dinner. On Sunday at noon, food was catered in at the Homestead. A large tent was put up for eating space with a lot of tables and chairs. The weather was ideal! There were cousins there I hadn't seen for over thirty-five years. What a great reunion it was!

With never a dull moment, Jeremy and his family drove up on Wednesday, August 15th. He asked to use my Saturn, which used to be his car. That way, Khaek had their car to visit her friends. Eric was here, too, so he and Jeremy spent time together. They brought the car back on Sunday evening, and we visited together until Khaek picked them up. Then they were off, driving back to Virginia. They took turns driving straight through the night, arriving back home at noon on Monday.

I was happy when Richard and Bob said they'd come up to help clean out my double garage in town, which had stuff in it yet from the previous owners. They came on the fourth Saturday of September. We gutted it out completely and pressure sprayed the floor. It was looking spic and span! On Sunday, when the floor was dry, I put the things back in the garage.

On the last day of work for the month of September, a cow stepped on my big toe. I went to see my doctor, and he put a splint on the toe. He gave me a hard shoe to walk in for support and for less toe movement. My comment to him was, "Just another battle scar!"

I had an unexpected trip to Watertown, Wisconsin. One afternoon, I was informed that my cousin, Lance, had died on October 13th. His funeral was held four days later. Again, as usual, I drove to Lanetta's home and we went together to Watertown. My cousin Sharon and Bob went with us, too. Another family get-together, but certainly one that wasn't planned.

I stopped working for Home Instead in the mornings. I only had the big farm job from noon to midnight now. I missed spending time with my clients, but it was for the best.

November came, and it was deer hunting time. Jeremy came from Virginia for the opening weekend of hunting. Years ago, there were a dozen or more hunters that would go together. Many of the guys weren't available anymore, so there were fewer hunters that year.

A few days later was Thanksgiving Day—turkey day! The traditional potato dumplings are only made once a year, and reserved only for Thanksgiving dinner. The day before, I'd be baking pies, usually from seven to nine pies total. I made more, because my kids liked to take a pie home with them. Evan, Christa and family, Richard, Bob, and Jeff were all there. Lanetta worked again, so she didn't come.

As the year wound down, with the month of December, everyone was in the Christmas spirit! Wow! Was I surprised by Jeff, when four days before Christmas, he came over with the truck, and on the back of it, there was a deep freezer. This was my Christmas present from my family. I was really happy to receive that!

Our Christmas Eve family get-together was at John and Lanetta's home. I stayed overnight and returned back home on Christmas Day. Back to work at noon the next day!

December 29th, I was going somewhere again; my car doesn't sit still long! I met Lanetta and Bob in Stevens Point, and from there, we drove together to Middleton, to the Marriott Hotel to attend the Junior State Holstein Banquet. My granddaughter, Shianne, Mary and Tom's daughter, was crowned Wisconsin Jr. Holstein Princess!

2008—Florida Bound

The year 2008 started out with purchasing airplane tickets for a trip to Florida from March 28th through April 1st with Lanetta, Bob, Mary and Sierra.

My work continued at the big farm, on the noon to midnight shift. It took me twenty-five minutes to get to work. I lived on the south side of Wausau, and had to drive through the city with the 25 MPH speed limit. Many times, it took longer, in winter especially, with the snow-covered, slippery roads.

Coming home from work on February 1st, I slid into the ditch. Thankfully, a fellow came by and helped me get out. This was after midnight when there isn't much traffic on the roads. I praised the Lord for His watchful care! It could have been so much worse.

It always seems to me that the months of January and February go by so fast. I don't get cabin fever because I'm always occupied with things to do! On weekends, going to church on Sundays, and oftentimes after, eating out with different folks, makes the majority of the days go by. Other times, I'd invite people over for dinner after church services.

The anticipation of waiting for the day to go on our trip was finally over! March 28th was here. It was 7:10 in the morning when Mary, her daughter Sierra, Bob, Lanetta, and I boarded our plane, ready to take off for Florida. We arrived in Florida at 2:30 in the afternoon, with the warm Florida sunshine welcoming us! We ate at a famous restaurant, Fish Bones, and afterwards got settled in.

Saturday, we spent time at Disney World; Sunday we were at Sea World; Monday, we went to Universal Studios. On Tuesday, a cab driver took us to Daytona Beach where we went swimming in the ocean, with its huge waves. We left the ocean site and traveled directly from there to the airport, where we were scheduled for our flight back home. We arrived home at 10:30 in the evening, leaving all our trip experiences behind, but having the memories with us for a lifetime!

On April 17th, Jeremy and his family went to the Mall of America. Jeff called me and said they would be coming by us the next day, and we made arrangements to eat together at the Blue Willow restaurant. It was a short and sweet visit, from which I left to go to work. Still, it was nice to see them briefly.

On Mother's Day, I went down to see Lanetta. Rich, Patti, Bob, and I met her at Fishtail Inn, a bar/restaurant near Lake Winnebago where she worked. We had dinner together there and the food was delicious.

Lanetta's employer also had a greenhouse. I was happy to take some flowering plants along back home with me. I couldn't buy any garden plants, because there wasn't any space for a garden at my home in the city, and what ground was there was very sandy. I did miss having my large garden!

June seems to be wedding month, and on Saturday, the 21st of June, I went to Lanetta's again. Together, we went to Jim and Nancy Stanelle's home to join in the celebration of their wedding. Jim is my first cousin on my mom's side of the relation. I stayed overnight at Lanetta's, spending the day with her.

This year, there was a change in our traditional date for the family reunion. Rather than having it on the last Sunday of July, it was held at a park in Fond du Lac on the second Sunday, July 13th. After the reunion, I attended stock car races with Lanetta in the evening, where her husband, John raced his car every week. This was my first time attending a stock car race. Talk about noise!

The next day, Lanetta and I attended the Dairy Promotion pot-luck dinner, held in appreciation for all the workers at the "Sundae on the Farm" event. I had off from work on Monday and Tuesday, which gave me the opportunity to stay over another night with her. The next day, we attended Farm Technology Days, which was held at a local farm. After a prolonged weekend, it was back to work on Wednesday.

My Story: Faith, Family, Farm

Marjorie and Victor, 2008

2008—Welcoming Victor

Another opportunity presented itself, and I wondered if it would work out. On August 5th, I attended a meeting held in our city library regarding the North Central Technical College CASS international student program. I liked the two main objectives of CASS: That the students learn marketable skills in a technical field of study; and that they be provided academic and social experiences which would lead to a better understanding of cultures, ideals, and ways of working together, and which they could share with their own countries upon returning home.

About a month previous, the person in charge of the program had come to my home and shared with me how great the need was for finding "host families" for the foreign exchange students who were coming to the US.

It was hard for me to picture how it would work out, even though I had room in my city home. With me working from noon to midnight, it would mean the student would be all alone with no family most of the day.

The supervisor indicated to me every home is different. Many a single parent has opened up their home for a student. But I thought at least on the farm, the boys were company for them. As a venture of faith, I consented to share my home with a foreign exchange student.

I received a packet of information about a Mexican boy. His name was Victor Ramirez Apolinas and he was nineteen. I would be his American mom, and as I called him, he'd be my little school boy, because he was so small in stature.

On August 12th, I was at the airport where all the host families were gathered to pick up their foreign exchange students. It was a bit difficult—they didn't know us, nor we them. All of a sudden in the distance, I saw a smaller guy with a name tag, "Victor". That was him! I went over and introduced myself, and gave him a hug.

One of the Mexican students who had been here for a year already explained to Victor, in Spanish, the situation at his new home, where I would be leaving for work before noon and arriving back home after midnight. I wouldn't be there when he returned home from school.

My knowledge of the Spanish language was very limited. However, as time went on, we learned to communicate very well with each other. When we drove into the garage the first time, his eyes opened wide as he saw the automatic door opener work. Where he lived in Mexico, their life style was very simple; no electric wash machines, no microwaves or the like. These were definitely new experiences for him. I was there in the morning to see him off to school, and he'd give me a hug. He called me "mum". The city bus picked him up three blocks away from the house.

I showed him things in the kitchen, and as he made himself feel "at home", I knew he liked to make his own food. We'd go shopping together, and he'd buy peppers, beans, cilantro, and all different types of Mexican foods. I became the recipient of some very good Mexican food!

On September 13th, there was a United Way parade in Wausau. The students took part in the parade, so I attended the event with Victor. Victor always went to church with me, too. He didn't have a Bible, so I purchased a Spanish/English Bible that was side-by-side on each page. He was really excited about it! It was hard for him to read English, but now at least, he could read his very own Bible, with Spanish alongside.

2008—Country Girl Once More

Across the road from the home farm was a house that was going into foreclosure. The folks had moved out in May, and a sheriff's sale was pending. Jeff called me one day and said, "We should buy it for hired help." The hired man and his family were living in an apartment in Merrill, and they were looking to move.

I thought it was a good idea, so I called my lender and discussed the purchase of the house on a three-acre parcel. The house was surrounded by all of the farm's cropland. Having a "city-slicker" move in could create problems, and besides, it would be ideal for the hired help!

Three days later, our lender came out to look at the house and property. We couldn't get into the house, it being locked, so we went to the farm across the road and sat at Jeff's kitchen table, talking for two hours about it all. Not knowing what price it would go for, the lender set a limit as to what he figured it would be worth.

On September 28th, Jeff called me again. The owner of the house had put a note on the door with the date for the Sheriff's sale, which was scheduled for October 8th at eight o'clock in the morning at the Marathon County Court House. Not knowing how a Sheriff sale is conducted, I decided to go to the Sheriff's Department to inquire about the sale procedure. I was told there would be bidding in the court house lobby. They gave me a sheet of paper, with all the information on it about the house.

It was October 8th, at 7:45 AM when I showed up in the court house lobby. No one was around! Then a gentleman with a business binder came, and asked if I was there for a sale. After I said yes, he asked me which one, because he had a number of them. "We'll start with the one you are interested in," he said. After waiting a little while, still no one came. They had a set price, upon which I needed to make a bid. After one bid, the house was mine!

On the last Saturday in October, the hired man's wife came and helped me clean it up, starting in the kitchen first; all the cupboards, of which there are many, then the stove and refrigerator, too. She was all excited about living in the country, and was especially happy for their two little boys! The family wanted to move in by the middle of November. Every chance I got, I'd go to the house and clean.

I received another phone call from Jeff, but this time, it wasn't about the house. He told me he thought he had a hernia again, so he went to see his doctor. His doctor said, "Yes, you're right." The surgery date was set for November 28th.

As if Jeff's last phone call wasn't enough, he called me several days later, on November 3rd to be exact, with not good news. The hired man had quit with no advance notice or communication to Jeff whatsoever!

Now what? I'd own two houses! I really didn't want to go into the rental business. It would have worked out well with the hired hand and his family, or so we thought.

On November 3rd, that same morning, I received word that I didn't have to go see Mary Ann anymore, a client through Home Instead that I had taken up in the past few weeks. I had helped her do laundry, cleaned her house, etc. I would go there, and then leave from her place to work at

113

the big farm, punching in at noon.

The morning had one undesirable phone call after another. Jeff's hernia, the hired man quitting, losing a client...we didn't see it then, but there is always a reason and a purpose for things happening, known only to God.

Back to the newly purchased country house...Victor's birthday was on November 8th, and we planned a birthday party for him out at the country house. We wanted to have a bonfire and a hayride; however, the falling rain dictated a change of plans. Instead, we heated up hot dogs on the old stove, along with all the other food, and the large birthday cake I had made. There were twenty of his fellow students there, along with their host parents.

We roughed it, because there wasn't much furniture in the house, only a large oak dining room table with five chairs, and a smaller table in the kitchen. The guys and gals sat in the living room on the carpet.

Lanetta came up the following Monday to help clean the country house. Whenever she came to see the house to help clean it, her comment was, "There is a lot of potential here." Then, Jeff's comment to me was, "Who would want to live in the city anyway?" Regardless of their comments and all my thoughts, the house was in shambles and needed work.

In fact, it needed a lot of attention; cleaning, and moving a lot of items out of it, many of which were still usable. We cleaned out the basement, and also got a good start on the garage. A furnace man was called out to look at the oil furnace. It was not in good condition. The repairs would have been costly, so the decision was made to have a new gas furnace installed. This was done in the beginning of December. Fortunately, it wasn't very cold weather yet. The new furnace was set on low, just high enough to keep the chill out of the house.

In 2008, Christmas was held at my house in the city. Busy I was - baking cookies, nut breads, and more for the family. We didn't do anything more in the country house till after the New Year.

Everyone came on Christmas Eve, and several of the grandchildren stayed overnight. I so looked forward to our family get-togethers, and so soon they were past. With the New Year beginning, my concentration was once again directed to the country house. It was purchased, and now became a project that consumed much of my time.

My Story: Faith, Family, Farm

Decisions

Decisions had to be made! I did a lot of praying for wisdom and direction. Being alone with so many obligations and responsibilities, there were many times I felt I was between a rock and a hard place, and couldn't go on. More and more, I realized I wasn't alone! God's mercy and His grace and His hand were at work in my life. I just needed to trust Him.

I had called a friend, Judy. She and her husband did interior painting. She came out to look at the rooms, and gave a cost estimate on it all. On January 10th, I met her at the house on my way to work. There was wallpaper above the kitchen cupboards, which she said we could take off.

Victor was such a blessing to me! He helped me scrape off the wallpaper in the kitchen. In the upstairs, while I was washing the ceilings and walls, Victor would be vacuuming the floors or scraping paint off of the baseboards.

Judy came to paint on January 20th. Before noon, on my way to work, I'd stop in and see how she was doing. The house was empty, so it was an ideal time to get everything painted. The walls had multiple nail holes in them, some places had wax on them, and there were cracks needing repairs all before the painting was done. Her color choices were a surprise to me, but she coordinated the rooms beautifully and I came to enjoy the environment the colors created.

Lanetta called me on February 5th, informing me that the house on our old farm, where I had lived for twenty-three years, had burned down. "It was a total loss," she said. The farm had just been purchased by a single fellow who was operating it. He wasn't home at the time of the fire, and its cause was never determined.

Life is ongoing and full of decisions! I had decided to have a real estate agent look at my house in town; and then afterwards, I showed her the country house. We discussed the potential of sales with both of them. She indicated the country house, being fixed up, would be an easy sale. Many people were looking for a house with a couple of acres out in the country. But, did I want to sell it?

Meanwhile, we continued work on the house. The kitchen cupboards' exterior was pine and places were chipped off, like veneer peeled off its backing. In February, I contacted the Kitchen Refacers. They came out, did some measuring, and gave me an estimated cost. I was asked to stop by their office for color and style choices.

Another large project was the bathroom. The previous owner had begun fixing the bathtub tile and was in the process of installing a shower head above the bathtub. It was left in the raw, a mess! I contacted a contractor to get it all fixed up. By the end of February, it was completed. Wow! It really looked nice!

In the beginning of March, my painter, Judy, came to help me pick out kitchen cupboard fronts and a countertop color. I leaned on her expertise in interior decorating. I had brought samples of cupboard refacing, countertop, knobs, and handles to the house so we could choose from amongst them.

The insides of the cupboards were solidly built. The undertaking of painting the entire inside was my job. I started painting on March 14th and was finished with all of them in a week.

There was more action at the country house in March! On March 23rd, I visited the local appliance store, which resulted in the purchase of a microwave, a new range, and a dishwasher. The kitchen workers said the appliances needed to be in the kitchen before they started on the cupboards. The microwave would be built in with the cupboards, directly above the range. The dishwasher was built in also. The kitchen was beginning to take shape!

The end of March was birthday time for me. Richard and Patti came to take me out for dinner. On that same day, after they left, I got ready to go to Lanetta's. She wanted me to come and help her clean her dad's trailer house. It was a Friday, and I arrived by her late in the evening. Early the next morning, we were "a-cleaning". We accomplished a lot, with just a little to finish at day's end.

On Sunday, Lanetta said we'd be going out to eat at noon. They were taking her husband's folks out to eat, too, for a late anniversary dinner, and for me, a late birthday dinner. We stopped at Walmart, then on to the supper club at 12:30. When we went to open the door to the dining area, my words were "Oh no!" Seated inside were forty-five to fifty people, and they all shouted, "Happy Birthday!" Yes, a surprise party, and successfully pulled off I might add.

Lanetta had invited so many people! Grace, the only other gal with me in all eight grades in school, was there together with her husband. Neighbors and cousins, and even Jeremy, Khaek, and the girls from Virginia! I had no idea they would be here. They were just in Wisconsin visiting two months ago. All my children were there; I couldn't hold back the tears. What a blessing to have so many wonderful family and friends! We all enjoyed a delicious family style dinner of chicken, ham, and all the trimmings. And I was even given many gifts; what a surprising and memorable day!

Seeing we didn't complete our cleaning on Sunday, we finished the job on Monday, after which I returned home for a cooperative meeting in the evening. Then, the next day I went back to work at the big farm!

On April 9th, I took off of work to go to Madison, along with another co-op director and our co-op manager. We went to speak personally with our state assembly representative about co-operative issues, and present our side of it all, for the benefit of cooperatives.

Back to the Country

Spring was bursting out all over—which meant it was lawn raking time! I was glad there wasn't much of a yard in the city; however, the country house made up for it. Victor and I did a lot of raking. There was an area with really long, dead grass (it never was a lawn). We got through it, so when grass mowing time came, there wouldn't be any surprise stumps or roots sticking up.

Progress was being made out at the country house. On April 6th, I stopped at the house on the way to work. The kitchen cupboards were getting their new face on.

In the middle of the month, the carpet store salesperson came out to measure the upstairs den and the stairs for the carpet I'd picked out. The kitchen flooring was worn down to the bare boards in front of the sink, and was replaced. The contractor put in the kitchen, the bathroom, and the laundry room floors, all in the same pattern of vinyl flooring. The house was really taking shape now.

It was birthday time for Jeff. Lanetta and Bob came up for his birthday dinner. I took off of work, and we enjoyed our time together at a fine restaurant in Wausau. It was a welcome break since I was spending a lot of time at the country house; not only time, but money, too. I enjoyed being out there, and believed in my heart that it was where I belonged. Yes, as time unfolded, it was the Hand of God and His Providence that brought me back to the country, with its wide-open fields. So the decision was made. Even though the housing economy wasn't very good at the time, I would sell the house in the city. I prayed toward that end that it would sell.

On May 6th, after three hours of visiting and business done, I signed a six-month contract with a real estate agent. The house in the city would be listed for sale. The transaction took place at the kitchen table in the city house. Many contracts and decisions are made at the kitchen table.

On May 8th, I bought a new riding lawn mower. It was a needed necessity, with so much grass to be mowed. Plus, it wasn't only all the work at the country house, but in the city, too, where the house had to be kept "spic and span" for the showings. I told Victor about it so he would keep his bedroom tidy. A showing of the house could be at any time; we never did get much advance notice.

Ah, but what a happy gal I was! Victor and I enjoyed planting a garden out at the country house. A neighbor of ours rototilled the ground for us and the area was just the right size. We planted tomatoes, broccoli, squash, green pepper plants, and Mexican peppers, for sure. We also planted seeds for lettuce, carrots, radishes, and onions. Now, it was time to watch it grow!

One of the elderly persons I was a caregiver for didn't live far from me in the city. Even after he was no longer my client through employment, I still kept in touch. Most every Sunday, I'd take him to church with me. Often times, I'd take him grocery shopping, too. Later, when he was not able to live alone, he entered a care center in Wausau. Victor and I would visit him, and he enjoyed it so much. He had two sons who didn't live in the area and they didn't come to visit. So, Victor and I made a point to visit as often as we could.

On May 31st, Victor moved out of my home. The students were required to live their last school year in an apartment on their own, since they'd spent the first year getting acquainted in a new country with their host family. I missed having him around. We used to go shopping together, and he always liked to help me. He certainly had been a big help to me at the country house!

We did keep in touch, though; I'd pick him up to go to church on Sunday mornings. At times, he'd come and stay with me on the weekend. I'd take him back on Sunday evening to his apartment right across the street from the college.

To the west of the country house, there were several acres of land that had grown up as tall grasses, and nothing was done with it by the previous owner. Jeff and I made a decision to put a fence around it and raise Holstein steers. Jeff would bring them over when they were several months old. In June, the pasture fence was finished and the grasses were grown up. Newcomers, a total of twenty-four steers, came over to make their home for a while.

Something was always going on! There was some problem with getting electric shocks on the outside water faucet on the back of the house. Every time the faucet was turned on, we'd get a shock. I had an electrician go through all the exposed wiring and fuse boxes to carefully check them out. Everything checked out good, and I was told to call our well person to have that checked out, too.

The well man came out the next day, and pulled the pump out. The wiring was the real old-fashioned kind, not rubberized. So, new wiring was needed and new piping. Both were originals from way back when the house was built. After having the new wiring and piping completed, we noticed that the water pressure wasn't very good. There wasn't much water coming through the pipes, and now with the steers drinking it, the volume usage was up.

I contacted the well man again and he suggested having the well hydrofractured. On July 1st, the work was completed, with three channels of water coming in. "You'll have a good water supply now," he said. He was right! Water just kept on a comin'!

A fast trip to Madison happened in July when I attended Uncle Joe's memorial service. I'll always remember Uncle Joe every time I drive my Lincoln town car, which I got from him.

On the 4th of July, I took my first shower in the country house. I brought good clothes along with me to change into since I was going to cut the grass and do work outside. It was a hot day, with me being sweaty, so the shower was welcomed! I had been invited to the neighbor's fiftieth wedding anniversary dinner in the later part of the afternoon. Not having to return to the city to get ready worked out great!

On July 11th, Rich came to help me clean the garage at the country house. We had everything taken out, all swept up, and ready to use the pressure washer. It was lunch time, and Rich went in the house to wash his hands. He came back out, saying there wasn't any water! He likes to kid around, so I didn't take him seriously.

I went into the house and turned on the faucet. No water! I couldn't believe it! I'd spent a sizeable amount of money and was told the water supply was very good.

I called the well man, and, it being a Saturday, he normally wasn't working. But, he happened to be not far from us just finishing a job and he said, "I'll be right over!" The problem was the underground wiring from the well to the house. He fixed it by laying new wire on top of the ground, to be buried at a later date. Thankfully, all worked out! The problem was fixed, and after lunch, Rich and I pressure sprayed the entire garage. Mission accomplished. All's well, when all works well!

On July 15th, an appliance truck backed up to the house to unload a new washing machine and dryer. They hooked up the hoses, vented the dryer, and plugged both appliances in. The laundry room was complete, ready for dirty laundry!

Slow but sure, I started to pack things in preparation for the move; sweaters in totes, blouses and slacks on hangers, and soon the closet was empty! Every time I'd leave for work, the car was packed full! I'd leave earlier, so there was time to unload it all into the country house before going to work.

Toward the end of the month, I received an estimate for work to be done in the basement. There weren't any floor drains, and an old chimney wasn't in use any more. Because it had bad cracks in the chimney basement wall, whenever it rained, a towel and pail were needed to just keep on soaking it up and squeezing it out!

I was told that it could be fixed so water would not come into the basement. It took the basement crew of two to get everything finished. They tore down the chimney, which was ground level in the front of the house, and hauled all the debris away. The basement was pressure sprayed clean; and since that time, it has been dry.

In the first section of the basement, indoor-outdoor carpeting was put in. This became an excellent place for the grandchildren to play with their Play-Doh and toys. The second section had a painted floor, and was used as the utility room. The furnace was in there, and an offset storage place had shelves with assorted items set on them.

Lanetta and Bob came to help take all the things out of the basement from the city house. There was a storage room down there, with "a lot of stuff" in it. We had both cars full a couple times as we hauled the stuff to the country house.

Moving Day

I turned the calendar to August, and saw it was family reunion time. The first Sunday in the month, I left early in the morning to see my relatives. After the reunion, I stayed overnight at Lanetta's. Arrangements were made with her that, on August 17th, a truck would be hired for moving all the large furniture, and she'd come up to help me.

A huge wind storm came through, which took a super big tree down. It was the kind of tree which would have made a great tree house with so many sturdy limbs. It fell over the driveway, so it had to be sawed up and removed. The tree trunk was located in a grassy area not kept up as lawn, and to this day, a section of the trunk is yet intact, with growth each year. It provides a cover for the donkeys, which were brought over to the country house from the farm. It was fortunate that the new fence wasn't built for the donkeys before the tree went down or it would have been severely damaged!

August 17th arrived—the big moving day! Lanetta had come up to help me the evening before. We were up early to empty my water bed mattress. The movers came at 10:30. They loaded all the big furniture onto the truck; it took seven and half hours to get it all moved. Thank you, Two

Men and a Truck!

Lanetta left late in the evening to go back home because she had to go to work the next day, and it was my first evening sleeping in my country house. Yes, the Providence of God! I was brought back to the country, with its wide-open fields.

Sold

After my move, Jeff went to Virginia for five days to visit Jeremy. It was really handy now, that I lived right across the road from the farm. I took off of work and did the milking. My ex brother-in-law stayed at the farm to help with chores while Jeff was gone.

At the end of the month, Saturday and Sunday, I emptied all the kitchen cupboards from the city house. Moving it all took two trips, with my car filled up both times!

It seemed there was always involvement outside of my own work! Hardy, the gentleman who I was a caregiver for, wanted me to be his health guardian. An attorney called me saying, "Marge, if you accept, there would be a hearing at the court house on September 9th."

So, I went to the hearing and Hardy came along as the Court appointed me as his health guardian. After the hearing, he came with me to see my new country home. We stopped in at the farm, and he got to see a calf born while we were there. After taking Hardy back to the Assistant Living Center, I returned to the farm to bottle feed the baby calves.

As I finished up with my work and left the barn, a terrible noise could be heard. I hollered for Jeff. Jenny was having her baby donkey, and the male was attacking her. Jeff jumped in the pen, and grasped the baby! The mom and baby were put into the cattle trailer. Males are known to kill the young when they are born, so I was glad that we were there to intervene!

On Sundays, I'd continue to pick Victor up at his apartment and we'd attend worship services together. He was happy to come out to the house, and take back with him some of the peppers, tomatoes, and broccoli we had planted together. He helped plant the garden, and now he could enjoy the fruits of his labor.

One Sunday evening, at sunset, we took a walk behind the house down to the pond. As we were walking, he said, "Mum, this is beautiful!" I won't ever forget his statement.

I answered back, "Yes, it is!"

Marjorie M. Beyersdorf

By the beginning of October, all things had been moved out of the city house. There were a few things left in the garage in town, along with my Lincoln town car, though. I had professional carpet cleaners come in to clean all the carpets. Being all cleaned up and windows washed, it was a daily prayer of mine that the city house would sell.

Friends Terry and Sue came to visit, (they used to be our neighbors years ago). They said, "Let's go get your things left in the garage in town!" They had come with their pick-up truck. I took them inside to see the house where I had lived in the city.

Cleaning is never done! Having accomplished all the cleaning of the house to be sold, now it was cleaning time on the farm. I had taken off work for a day, to do extra special cleaning of the barn milk pipeline, and to do touch-ups in the milk house. Two days later, the state inspector came and gave good comments!

On the last day of October, the real estate agent called and said, "I've got an offer to purchase the house!" Two days later, she came to my home and we had the Option to Purchase papers signed. After coming together on figures, she came to my workplace on November 4th to sign the final papers. It needed to be done right away, in order for the buyers to get their first-time home buyers rebate.

Praise the Lord! He answers prayer in His time! The six-month contract with the real estate agent was to expire two days later, on November 6th. Houses weren't selling well at all because of the economic conditions. I was so thankful I didn't have to go through winter with heating the house, sidewalks to shovel, taxes, insurance, and all the responsibilities in general!

November 8th was Victor's birthday. After church services, guests were invited over for a birthday dinner. I wrapped his present in one box after another, smaller boxes always getting larger. He had to open ten boxes in all. How exciting and fun it was to watch him! In the evening, his roommates and host parents had pizza and birthday cake at his apartment. Yes, he had two birthday parties!

When the garage was cleaned, all things "no good" had been thrown on a pile outside. Before the snow came, we needed to get it out of there! The Monday after Victor's parties, Lanetta came to help haul all that junk away.

The Lincoln car was yet to be brought to the country house, so Lanetta and I went to bring it home and put it in the clean garage—its "new home" now. On November 9th, I left the driveway for the last time with my memories of being a "city gal" for a little over three years!

My Story: Faith, Family, Farm
Thrown by a Cow

The weather was really warm for this time of the year, which was really great for us! Jeff had the neighbor dig a trench for an underground water line from the house to the steers' new heated water fountain. Prior to this, the animals drank out of a water tank with a float in it, which wouldn't work out in winter; it would freeze. The following day after the trench digging, it was Thanksgiving Day. Rich and Bob came up to enjoy turkey and dumplings with Jeff and I. What a year to offer special thanks!

I flipped the calendar to December and we got an early start for Christmas. Jeff and I went to our neighbors' tree farm to cut down our Christmas trees. Usually, we didn't do that till the second or even the third week of December. After our co-op Christmas party on December 6th, I was home early to set the tree up in the living room, put the lights on, and finish trimming it. I was happy to have that accomplished.

On December 9th, we had our first snowstorm of the year. Jeff brought the truck over for me to take to work, because it had four-wheel drive and my little Saturn couldn't make it up the driveway! I took him back home and went to work.

The next day, I kept the truck to go to work, but it was a short day! After an hour and a half, I was walking through an exit area from the older milking parlor as cows were coming out. One of them started to come at me, but I didn't take her seriously. I pulled my hand shocker from my pocket to ward her off, but that shocker meant nothing to her. It went flying; my cap flew, and I flew, landing on my left side on the cement! At that moment, as I'm lying there in pain, my phone rang, and it was Jeff. "Mom, are you busy?" How ironic.

After I hung up with Jeff, I called for my foreman. He said, "Stay right there. I'll come get you." My employer said to me a few minutes later to "go home; take a hot bath and some aspirin." I was helped into my truck, and I had called ahead to Jeff to come help me into the house. Never will I forget that night! Throughout the evening, I had such intense pain.

After telling Lanetta the next morning what happened, she said, "You need to see a doctor, if I have to come up and take you myself!" Then I called my employer at the big farm in the morning and said, "I need to see a doctor." One of the farm employees came to take me to the clinic. X-rays were taken of my left side, showing the femur bone pushed up a little into the hip socket. Describing it to me, the doctor said it was like "pushing ice cream down on a cone." The doctor wasn't sure about a femur bone fracture, so he ordered me to see another doctor.

Considering that it was the weekend (Friday), an appointment was set for Monday, the 14th of December. I couldn't put weight on my left foot, so on the way home from the doctor's office, a walker was purchased for me.

During the weekend, I received a phone call from Amy, a gal from church. She said, "My husband was helping out at the neighbors' place, and was told a lady got hurt at the big farm. That wasn't you, was it, Marge?"

I said, "Yes, it was."

She offered to help me in whatever way she could. She was "God's Angel." She took me to my doctor's appointment on Monday. After more X-rays were taken, a surgeon came into the exam room and said, "Young lady, you need surgery!" What could, or should, I say? All pre-surgery tests were taken, blood work drawn, and an electrocardiogram done. Surgery was scheduled for four o'clock the next day.

In between all this, before going to the hospital, the real estate agent picked me up with my walker, and we went to the County Land and Title office. We had to sign papers for transfer of the title, which was the final sale transaction on the city house. She brought me back home, and Amy picked me up an hour and a half later to take me to the hospital. She stayed with me before and after surgery.

In the hospital, the day after surgery, my doctor said, "Everything checks out good. If you have someone to stay with you, you can go home." Amy came to get me in the evening and then stayed with me overnight. She put my Christmas decorations up, which I had laid out but didn't get up due to the accident. There was a reason the tree went up earlier than usual, but I didn't know why at the time.

The children were calling to see how I was doing, and I told them all I was fine. Amy picked up a prescription for me the next day. She left after lunch to be with her family. Another friend, Lisa, brought food over in the afternoon. I could see God's Hand in it all!

The morning of December 23rd, two days before Christmas, Amy took me to see my doctor to get checked over and to take the stitches out. Lanetta and Mary came in the afternoon. They got busy getting the food and all the preparations ready for Christmas Eve day, when we'd all be together. But there were no Grandma's Christmas cookies this year.

Mary stayed overnight with me on Christmas Eve. We watched *It's a Wonderful Life* together. She left in the afternoon, to be with her family on Christmas Day.

From here on in, it meant I wouldn't be going to work for a while. So it ended a "full", "eventful", and "on-going" year!

My Story: Faith, Family, Farm
Hardy

Since my accident, spending time in the house was now routine for me. I took advantage of that extra "sitting" time by cleaning desk drawers out and sorting through all the files in the filing cabinets.

On January 2nd, 2010, I received a call from the local hospital that the elderly man I was a caregiver for, Hardy, had been brought into the hospital. I was informed that the next morning he would be transferred to the Marshfield Hospital, where he was to have surgery to place a trachea in his throat. He had a hard time swallowing, and it was increasingly getting worse. Tests revealed there were signs of cancer. I was consulted, due to having his health power of attorney. January 5th was his surgery day.

I had a co-op district directors meeting at Medford from nine in the morning till three-thirty in the afternoon. It was my first venture out since my accident. I drove to the meeting, and afterwards, went to the hospital in Marshfield. Hardy was just being wheeled into his room when he saw me sitting in there. His eyes opened wide, he was so happy!

On January 13th, he was brought back to the Rehabilitation and Nursing Center in Wausau. Because I wasn't able to be at work yet, I spent time with him. I'd pick him up and take him to see his family doctor. His physical condition was getting worse. Due to medications he was on, he'd be very sleepy. His doctor's nurse scheduled radiation treatments for his throat.

On February 12th, the decision needed to be made on whether or not to continue treatments. There was a meeting of Hardy's nurse, his doctor, myself, and a hospice worker. I would be the one to sign the papers to place him in hospice care. I called his family doctor and discussed the matter. Hardy couldn't eat, and he was on a lot of pain medication, due to the pain and discomfort, so I did sign the papers. Later, his family physician said to me, "You did the right thing. He would have wanted that done."

I received a phone call from the Rehabilitation and Nursing Center that Hardy had died at eight-thirty in the evening, just five days after he was in hospice care. The call came while I was traveling home from Wednesday evening prayer service. I'm thankful to have helped him during the latter part of his life here on earth. I've several letters from him, one of which I treasure, where he thanked me for sharing about Jesus, who was now his Savior, too. He expressed such appreciation, for all I had done for him.

I went to the funeral home on Saturday evening. The next day after church services, Victor and I attended the memorial service for Hardy, which was held in the funeral home. While I sat there, I remembered all the times I had spent with Hardy; one time in particular, when Hardy wanted to go for a drive. He wanted to show me the area where his home was; we also drove by the church, with the cemetery nearby. I looked at his gravesite and the monument stone, with his name on it. I praise the Lord, he is with Jesus now!

Always On the Move

In February, my painter came and painted the three bedrooms upstairs, the den, and the stairway. She had completed the downstairs painting a year ago.

For four months, I had rented the bedrooms out to a co-worker whose wife had placed a restraining order on him, done rather abruptly. Having no place to go, I told him, he could interim at my house. I wasn't even living there yet, I was still in the city. He lived there from July through October, and I moved to the country in August. His four children would come out on weekends. He worked days, and I worked noon to midnight, so we hardly saw each other, except on weekends.

At work, he had shared with me about him and his wife not getting along. I told him they would be in my prayers, and if I could help in any way I would. I believe in putting action with prayer, therefore offered him the opportunity to live in my house. With the upstairs rented out, the painting was left to a later date.

In the end of February, Jeremy, Khaek, and the girls came to visit. Jeremy had seen the house when it hadn't looked good, before any fixing up was done. Seeing it now, he was surprised. "Wow!" he said. "It really looks different; really great!" They visited friends. Jeremy stayed with Jeff, and Khaek by her folks, and they stopped in by me on Sunday afternoon again before heading back home to Virginia.

Always on the move I was! Lanetta came up on March 1st to help get my things, which had been left at the farm when I moved from there. She helped me fix the fireplace with cement blocks. We always had a good time working together! She stayed overnight, and left after lunch the next day.

March 3rd was my first day back to work since my accident. I had lost my career of working with cattle, since the doctor had ordered me not to work with them, in fear of my getting hurt again. I was put in the repair shop instead, sorting out nuts and bolts, putting them in their proper bins. The whole month of March, I spent getting back in the groove of working and punching the clock again. The work hours now were eight in the morning till four o'clock.

My Story: Faith, Family, Farm

Birthdays were always a special day for my family, so Richard and Patti came up for my birthday. We went out to eat at Pizza Hut. Jeff came with us, too. Afterwards, we enjoyed birthday cake and ice cream at home, along with looking at old pictures from years past.

With my birthday being at the end of March, spring time is always welcomed in around the same time! The turn of the calendar to April meant it was here. I started to rake the lawn a little at a time. My accident had slowed me up a bit. In fact, at the end of March, I had several appointments with my chiropractor. There was so much pain right above my hip. The chiropractor cut my working hours down from eight to four hours. I was seeing him twice a week.

I still kept going though, just pacing myself. Spring was barn cleaning time. I didn't have time to sit around. The white-washer came and whitened it up! My job was to wash the barn windows after the white-washing was completed. Inspection from the state inspector was on April 15th, and it came back as a Grade A report. It was always good to work in a clean environment, and have our hard work recognized as such.

On April 23rd, it was birthday time for Jeff. I baked him a cake, and on the way to work, took it over to him. The following weekend, April 30th, (I didn't work Saturdays or Sundays) my nephew, Mike came to my house, and together, we went down by Mary and Tom's farm. We helped them put in a new waterbed mattress. Later, we went in their woods to pick morels (mushrooms).

I had taken off work on Monday, too, and before leaving Mary's on Monday, we went to Sierra's high school. She had a horticulture class and she wanted me to pick up some of their flowers and vegetable plants. We left with a carload of plants. I had my work cut out for me to plant them all. Mike stayed overnight at my house and left early in the morning when I went off to work.

A few weeks later, winter made a comeback! During the evening of May 7th, three inches of snow fell. It was a surprise to wake up to the sight of all the snow on the ground. Good thing I didn't have anything planted outside because it surely would have frozen.

I took Victor shopping to buy him a nice suit, shirt, and tie for his graduation. This was a new experience for him. He had never owned a suit before, and he looked sharp in it! Victor's graduation day was May 15th. After the college graduation program, we all ate at the Elk's Club. In the evening, there was a party at the Columbus Club, with all the pizza you could eat.

The last week of May, Victor and his roommates had to clean their apartments. Each student went to live with their host parents for their last month in America. Victor took some extra classes, so I'd drop him off at school before going to work. I'd pick him up again around four-thirty in the afternoon to go shopping together again, this time to buy a suitcase set for him. He would be going home with much more than what he came to the US with him.

During the month of May at work, they had me doing a lot of painting of the house foundation, gates, and posts outside. At home, I was busy planting flowers, and then my garden.

As I looked around one day, it occurred to me it seemed like "stuff" always accumulates, especially in the garage! I took everything out of the garage, and covered it with a canvas in case of rain. Two days later, I pressure-washed the floor and the bottom part of the walls. After the garage was dried out good, all the things were put back in.

On June 19th, I was on the way to Lanetta's. I helped her clean her dad's trailer house. Mary came too, and we both stayed overnight at Lanetta's. The following day, Sunday, was Father's Day. We went to the June dairy breakfast at a farm in Outagamie County. Rich and Patti met us there, and it was a fun family affair. Mary left for home on Sunday evening. Bob, Lanetta, and I enjoyed the stock car races in Seymour where John was racing.

Weeding the garden and the flowers, and cutting grass all kept me busy in between my job, helping Jeff, and keeping up the house. On June 26th, the group of students and their host parents were all invited for a final party at our place. Having the garage cleaned out was nice, and we spread out the food and set it up out there. I made potato salad, salads, and desserts. Two of the guys grilled the brats and hot dogs. It was a good time for all! The last of the guests left at eleven o'clock in the evening.

The next day, I took Victor to the airport. We had to say good-bye with tears in our eyes. Victor said, "Mum, I will come visit you again sometime!" As I drove home from the airport, I thanked God for the time and experiences we had shared together.

I remembered when he first came, how he didn't know English and that I knew very little Spanish. I wanted to portray to him the language of love. I drew three crosses on the palm of my hand, one large one, centered between two small ones. I looked up and said, "Jesus loves you, He loves me, and I love you," and I gave him a hug. He smiled and he hugged me right back. Such had been the start of our American "Mum-Son" relationship.

Today he still continues to e-mail me and calls me by phone on my birthday, Thanksgiving, and Christmas. He states his family is all doing well, and wishes our family well, too!

My Story: Faith, Family, Farm
Another Summer

My brother, Richard, and his friend, Mary, were coming this year for the family reunion at our cousin's farm, north of Appleton, Wisconsin the last Sunday in July. So in preparation, I made sure the bedroom upstairs would be ready for them. The windows needed washing; the flies had been busy leaving their marks. Afterwards, I put up new curtains, which I had, but never did get them hung until now.

They stayed overnight with me, and on Monday, we went to visit Mike (my brother's son) who lives in Suring. We drove through the Indian Reservation on the way home, stopped in Shawano, and had our evening meal together. What a memorable day!

After having breakfast together the following morning, they left for the airport to catch their flight back home to Arizona. Time always seemed so short when we were together. I treasure the days with the experiences we have when they come to visit!

Since my work accident at the end of last year, I was still experiencing pain above my left hip. My chiropractor referred me back to the Bone and Joint Clinic. I made an appointment, and the doctor there ordered physical therapy for me. So, starting in August, I went to physical therapy three times a week.

August 17th marked the one-year anniversary in my country house. I have so much to be thankful for!

The last Saturday in August, I was on my way to Mary's to help her to do extra cleaning and baking together. We made our favorite cinnamon sweet rolls, strudels, and bars. In the evening, we went out to Pizza Hut. On Monday, we did the kitchen cleaning, and Tuesday afternoon I left for home. Mary's kids were always happy when Grandma came!

On September 8th, I had a former neighbor, Ede, over for lunch. She had moved to Georgia in the early '90s. I invited my next door neighbor, Esther, over too. We had a lot of visiting to catch up on! I recalled when our family moved to Wausau in the late 70s, Ede and Esther were the first to visit and welcome us into the neighborhood.

My last physical therapy appointment was on September 20th. A week later, I took a physical evaluation. The appointment took from 12:45 to 4:00—what a workout! They created a report of my capabilities to send to my employer.

It was so handy having a Christmas tree farm across the road; it made it so easy for me to get evergreen boughs. With our pickup truck, I'd get a load of them and put them all around the foundation of the house. They made a nice wintery scene by dressing up the outside of the house, especially when the snow came and the boughs showed really well, with a white frosting effect!

Soon it was deer hunting time! Jeremy and my ex brother-in-law were here visiting for the hunting season. Thanksgiving Day brought the family together here, for our turkey and dumpling dinner, with all the trimmings. The hunters always enjoyed the good, hot food after a long day in the woods.

I was starting to hear Christmas songs on the radio. We had our co-op Christmas dinner on December 2nd. I was busy getting a Christmas letter ready, trimming the house, and doing all the baking, besides my job and helping Jeff on the farm! The time before Christmas always seemed to go by fast!

I'd never driven to Rhinelander before, and my first trip there was for a required appointment with a State vocational rehabilitation consultant, Michael J. Guckenberg. It was definitely a new experience heading north! After hearing of my life and work history, as I told him, he said "Girl, with your memoir, you should write a book!" Often times, it was in the back of my mind to do, so to Mike I said, "Thanks for igniting a spark of thought!" Seeing him was one year to the day that my accident had happened.

Two weeks later, December 24th, the whole family came together in my home. Lanetta always brings food and snacks, and this year, she made all preparations. Mary stayed overnight, but everyone else left late in the evening. Mary's oven wasn't working, so she wanted to do some baking by me for her to take home. Not the usual happening on Christmas Day! But, we did have a fun time baking together. Cinnamon sweet rolls, cherry strudels, bars, and even some Christmas fudge, all went home with Mary when she left in the late afternoon.

2011—Month by Month

How often we take things for granted; things like a good voice! First, I had a cold, and soon after, my voice went. I had an acute case of laryngitis, which stayed with me for a couple days. I wasn't able to go to work, so the beginning of the new year of 2011 found me resting more and drinking fluids to rid myself of such a nasty cold.

In the month of January, there were several co-operative board meetings. The co-op manager had resigned, so extra meetings were held to look into hiring a new manager, or at the very least, an interim manager, plus make plans for 2011.

I had a frightening experience one day with my car when I heard a loud bang! "What was that?" I said out loud.

As I was backing the car up in my yard, a front spring had broken and pierced the left front tire which blew the tire with a loud bang. Was I thankful that it didn't happen on the road while I was driving; and also thankful for Jeff, who'd always been very skillful in fixing cars, tractors, or whatever else breaks!

At work, I was cleaning and polishing stainless steel in the large milking parlor, which was open to the public five days a week. People could view the milking procedures from above by going up on a set of stainless steel winding stairs, which were cleaned daily. My hours working at the big farm had changed again and were now four hours on Monday, Wednesday, and Friday from eight till noon. Then on Tuesday and Thursday, I would work six hours, from eight till two.

At the end of March, on my birthday, Lanetta, Bob, and I went to visit my grandson, Dwayne. He had purchased his own farm near the village of Wonewoc. This was our first visit to see his milking parlor, the cows, and the whole set-up! He was excited to show us the entire farm! While there, I received a phone call from Victor in Mexico, calling to wish me a "Happy Birthday!"

I finished working on my records for taxes, and it was a good job accomplished! I took the files to the tax preparer on April first. Then from April 14th through the 18th, Jeff went to visit Jeremy and his family in Virginia. The hired man and I did all the chores. Jeff also had an extra person come in to do the milking.

Easter was a little later this year and Jeff was back in time to enjoy it with us. Bob, Lanetta, Rich, Jeff, and I all enjoyed a grill-out of rib eye steak at my place. Rich is a master griller, and grilled them to perfection!

I attended a bridal shower on May 6th for Nichole, who would be my granddaughter-in-law and Dwayne's wife once they married. The shower was held not far from Mary's farm, so afterward, I planned to stay overnight at Mary's. In the evening, Mary took me to her daughter Shannon's new house in Sun Prairie. On Monday, we went looking for morels in their woods. Then finally, in late afternoon, I left for home after a full, event-packed weekend!

Mid-May, the neighbor came to rototill my garden. Another year to plant a garden—which I so enjoyed doing! The rhubarb had really grown up, so it was time for the first rhubarb torte of the season. My favorite! Oh how great are the blessings of spring and summer!

"Mom, can we come up?" Lanetta asked over the phone one day. She and her employer surprised me with a visit on May 23rd by coming up with a trailer to buy a donkey. Her employer owned one donkey and a llama, but the llama had died the evening before; and the donkey was beside itself with grief, so she wanted another partner for it. I sold her one of my female donkeys, making sure the other one would be happy now.

Dwayne and his bride Nichole were married on July 9th. I drove to Lanetta's, and we went together to the wedding. The ceremony was held at Stoney Creek Resort, in the Dells area. We stayed overnight at the resort, but had to leave earlier than we planned to on Sunday.

Unfortunately, Lanetta's car brakes went out, and we couldn't drive home without brakes! She called for a tow truck, which took us up to where John was waiting for us with his racing trailer in Waupun. It was an unexpected way to go home after the wedding! I stayed overnight at Lanetta's and left for home Monday afternoon.

More Road Trips

Several times a month, it seemed my car and I were on a road trip! The last Sunday of July was family reunion time on my mother's side of the relation. We had a fun time, with our cousins in Fond du Lac in charge of planning this time. We did something different; we played bingo for prizes. The weather wasn't too hot, making it a comfortable and really good time together!

Family get-togethers were often this year! I went to my aunt's funeral service in Appleton. It was a trip there and back home in one day.

Plus, several times a year I'd go down to visit Mary's farm. This time, I'd left on Friday, August 26th after work. We *always* did cleaning together! On Saturday, we went to Dwayne's farm, a forty-five-minute drive from Tom and Mary's farm. We helped Dwayne do the evening milking in the parlor. Nichole always helped, but that evening she was attending a friend's bachelorette party. I spent Sunday with Mary, leaving late Sunday evening, because we wanted to finish shampooing the living room and dining room carpets.

Monday morning, at eight o'clock, I was back on my job. Plus, I had a project going on at home; I was painting my basement walls in between all else that was going on!

It was corn on the cob time! Sweet corn was ready to be picked; some to eat, some to sell, and a lot to freeze, but not all for me. My grandchildren

My Story: Faith, Family, Farm

liked the corn. Their comments were always, "We like Grandma's homemade sweet corn!"

Lanetta came up to visit on October 3rd and stayed overnight. We were always helping each other! She helped me move things from the basement and out to the garage. Oh no! The garage was filled with stuff again!

A few weeks later, I learned from my cousin Kaye that she was writing a book, and I told her that I was looking for an editor.

On October 22nd, Kaye and her daughter came to visit and stayed overnight. What a fun time we had together! We toured Jeff's farm, and I showed them all of the calves. Then, we went home to my place and I set up a guest room for each of them. It was nice having people in the house to cook for, and I really enjoyed the visit with them!

My granddaughter, Shannon, had been making plans to get married in Jamaica on February 29th of next year. Lanetta called and said, "I'm planning on going to the wedding, and you should go, too." We were all invited. The cruise and flight tickets had to be purchased soon, so my decision had to be made—yes or no!

I didn't really want to go, never having been on a cruise before, but I knew they all wanted me to come along. And as convincing as they were, I agreed to join a group of seventeen family members to see Shannon get married.

Meanwhile, at work, I was busy cleaning filters on each individual milking machine. There are one hundred milking machines, and each one has two small air filters. My job was cleaning two hundred filters and one hundred pulsators.

We had our annual Co-operative meeting on November 17th. The board elected me as their secretary. We were going through a lot of discussion and studies on merging with another cooperative.

Thanksgiving Day came this year on November 24th. We had the dining room seats all taken! Jeremy, Khaek, and the girls were there, with cousin, John, Mary, Rich, Bob, Jeff, and me.

On Thanksgiving evening, Mary took me with her on a new experience. At midnight, we went to "Black Friday" sales. That sure was something! It was crazy! So many people in the wee hours of the morning, and all shopping! One store was handing out Five Hour energy shots. (Mine is still in the cupboard today—I never drank it.) Mary wanted to get a good deal on a laptop computer for her daughter, Sierra, who would be starting at the University of Wisconsin-Madison.

Two days after Thanksgiving Day, I made another Thanksgiving dinner! My two grandsons couldn't come on Thursday, and Lanetta wasn't able to either. So, she and Bob, along with the boys, came for dinner; another full dining room table! Lots of food, family, and fun rounded out our time from

Thursday through the weekend!

My thoughts then turned toward Christmas and making plans for what needed to be done. Baking cookies was done earlier this year because we were going to visit Dwayne and Nichole on their farm on December 17th. I wanted Christmas cookies to take with me to give to them. Again, I drove to Stevens Point, and from there, we went the rest of the way, Lanetta, Bob, and I.

Three days later, on December 20th, I went to my home town, Forest Junction, to attend the memorial service of one of our neighbors there. Her boys and mine, being the same ages, had been very close friends.

With all the previous events, Christmas Eve crept up fast! The family came; the excitement was there in exchanging gifts, and in sharing the Christmas Eve observance together. Late in the evening, everyone but Mary left for home. She stayed with me until the 27th, and we enjoyed our hours together.

The Jamaican Wedding in 2012

Knock, knock, knock, a New Year enters in—2012! And so, we started another year all over. It was birthday time for Mary on January 7th. I met Bob in Stevens Point, and he went along with me to "surprise" Mary on her special day! It was a three-hour drive one way and sure made for one full day! I baked a birthday cake ahead of time, and we stopped to purchase chicken for a meal together—memories in the making!

Mondays were Lanetta's day off from work. She came up by me the first Monday in February and we went shopping together to get some clothes for the Jamaica wedding cruise. We would be leaving the dock of New Orleans on the 25th of February.

I had mixed feelings about going! I'd been on an airplane many times, but if something happens to the plane, you can't get out and fix it. If the big cruise liner has a calamity, what would I do? I don't know how to swim! On the highway in a car, it isn't much safer! I'm thankful I know the Lord Jesus. "My time is in His Hands" from Psalms 31:15 is one of my favorite verses. It's a walk of faith in Him each day!

The awaited trip came, and I was ready to go. I left early in the morning on February 25th to drive to Lanetta's. Her husband took us to the airport in Milwaukee. Bob, Lanetta, and I met Mary, Sierra, Shannon, and Gabe

(Shannon's future husband) at the airport. We stayed overnight at the Country Inn in New Orleans. Gabe's relatives were there. Together, we had a pizza party and got acquainted with each other.

Sunday morning, we left the dock and it was out into our adventure at sea! We headed for Montego Bay, Jamaica, for Shannon and Gabe's wedding ceremony. It took us three days to get there. The couple said their vows on the sandy beach with the Caribbean Sea as a backdrop.

One day later, after the wedding, we were on the way to visit the Cayman Islands. Our last stop was on Friday at the Mexican Cozumel Island, after which, the ship headed toward New Orleans to dock. After an eventful week, it was good to know the cruise was over, and I was headed back to dry land again.

Saying good-bye to the sea, we went directly to the airport and arrived back in Milwaukee after having departed there one week ago! John was waiting to pick us up and we headed for home. I stayed overnight at Lanetta and John's, and a week later, I was driving home. I stopped at the post office to pick up my mail on the way—a whole grocery bag full!

Tuesday morning, it was back to work at the big farm! I was cleaning and polishing stainless steel in the milking parlor, plus also painting with epoxy paint on the walls and floors in the newly built medical center.

The March co-operative meeting was held on the evening of my birthday. As a treat, I brought a homemade birthday cake to share with the board members.

Right before Easter, I was usually busy making éclairs, as it always seemed to be the tradition to do so. The family came for Easter dinner, and Rich was again the grill master for the delicious steaks!

As good as our time together was, with all the good food, it would be empty without the celebration of the resurrection of Christ. In 1 Corinthians 15:55-57, God's Word says: "O death, where is thy sting? O grave, where is thy victory? The sting of death is sin; and the strength of sin is the law. But thanks be to God, which giveth us the victory through our Lord Jesus Christ." We need not fear death; His victory becomes ours through a relationship with Christ as we live out our daily lives trusting in Him.

The weather was unusually warm for the time of year. Temperatures were in the 70s! Even the tree buds were opening early! That meant no apples for the year, because a later freeze inevitably came and that was the end of the blossoms.

In April, Jeff went to New York to visit Eric. He wanted to see the "Big Apple" before Eric moved a few months later. Jeremy met them, and together they went sightseeing around the big city. The hired man and I did milking and chores on the farm while Jeff was gone, along with me feeding the milk bottle calves as usual.

In May comes Mother's Day! Rich and Patti drove up to take me out to eat, and Jeff joined us, too. A week later, Mary had a meeting in town and came for a visit. After an overnight stay, she left for home in the morning.

May 28th brought granddaughter Sierra's high school graduation. The ceremony was held at the River Valley High School in Spring Green, Wisconsin. The following day, I attended the graduation of a family member with whom I knew from the fellowship at church. The parents home-schooled their children and had a really great graduation time for their son, held in their garage, with a noon dinner, a program, and all!

When Shannon and Gabe were married in Jamaica in February, not all the relatives went on the cruise, so on June 9th, they held a wedding reception at their home in Sun Prairie. Tents were set up, with food and beverages, and it was a good family time together! There was visiting and watching the wedding video, too.

One Event After Another

June 24th was an exciting day for me! I went to "Sundae on the Farm" in Calumet County, an event that Lanetta puts a lot of work into organizing. The real excitement was meeting my brother and his friend, Mary there! They were visiting some friends of theirs in Appleton and wanted to attend the farm event. Afterwards, they followed me back home and stayed with me through Wednesday morning. They then drove to Appleton to take their rented car back and to board the plane for their flight home to Arizona.

The very hot and humid weather was upon us! I kept busy with weeding and cutting the grass, plus all the daily routine chores, besides my job where I'd punch in at the big farm.

The family reunion this year was held the first Sunday in August at a campground in Forest Junction. I attended and stayed overnight after the reunion at Lanetta's, returning home late Monday evening.

Sierra's belated high school graduation party was planned for August 18th. My nephew, Mike, drove along with me to Mary's. We went a day early to help set the tent up and get the table and chairs from a neighboring church. We helped with food preparation, a fruit bowl, and I also made deviled eggs. The weather cooperated, and it was a great day had by all!

My car hardly ever sits still! On August 25th was Rich's stepson Dan's and his bride Brittany's wedding day in Green Bay. So, off I went to that!

September and October meant harvest time was here again. Corn silage chopping, and corn and soybean combining kept farmers busy! For me, I was finishing up with the garden for another year, and freezing the last of the sweet corn. With a lot of garden produce, I had a harvest dinner for two families from church, along with our pastor and his wife. October is Pastor Appreciation month. What better way to show appreciation in word and deed than by inviting them out to dinner?

The air outside was getting crisp and cold. On October 25th, all the flowering plants came into the house. That evening, the temperature dropped to twenty-five degrees, our first killing frost. The dining room turned into my greenhouse once again!

On November 9th, I left for Mary and Tom's farm. I met Shannon on the way and she gave me a turkey to take back with me, to prepare for our Thanksgiving dinner. Shannon's mother-in-law raises turkeys, and the large turkey she gave me weighed twenty-six pounds!

While down by Mary, we cleaned the house. Then on Friday evening, we went out for a fish fry. On Saturday, we were washing walls, picture hanging, and doing some cleaning in the kitchen, too. The grandkids know Grandma's specialty is cleaning!

On Sunday, we went to an apple orchard nearby to get apples to take along back with me. I left early evening on Sunday, arriving back home, safe and sound, at eight forty-five. Another full weekend!

Marjorie M. Beyersdorf

Christmas Dinner, 2012

Vacation Time for Christmas

I had two weeks' vacation I hadn't used, so my employer said, "Take off, and use them up!" If I didn't use them up before December 1st, I would lose them. So, I got to do a lot of extra work at home. The annual project of putting evergreen boughs around the house was finished earlier than in past years. I finished cleaning the house and getting it ready for Thanksgiving Day, and for the family coming.

My grandson Evan, his wife Christa, and their family, plus Gabe and Shannon, Rich, Bob, Lanetta, Mary, Jeff, and I were all around our Thanksgiving table that year. We had a family discussion after our meal about doing something different for Christmas, such as exchanging names for gifts. Never had we done it before. "Let's do it, and see how it works out," I said. Names were exchanged on Thanksgiving Day.

As the song-writers wrote "Silver Bells", Christmas was in the air! December comes and goes fast, because we take on so many things.

On December 8th, I went to the tree farm across the road from my house to select a Christmas tree. That finished, it was time to start writing my yearly Christmas letter. It took time, addressing around seventy-five envelopes and writing a personal note on the back side of each one. I enjoy sharing and writing the true meaning of Christmas! Christmas can only be truly celebrated if we know and have accepted the One whose birth we celebrate.

Even as the angels said on the hillside to the shepherds tending their sheep, "Fear not for behold, I bring you good tidings of great joy, which shall be to all people. For unto you is born this day in the city of David a Savior, which is Christ the Lord" (Luke 2:10-11).

Giving, sharing in His Love, gifts at Christmas, Christmas cookies, making our time available, and helping meet the needs of others...that's Christmas to me! God set the example. "He so loved the world that He gave his only Son!"

On December 24th, Christmas Eve day, I had to work in the forenoon. Upon arriving back home, everyone was by my place already. I came into the living room, and didn't even notice it right away. The family had bought a new flat screen television as my gift. Because I wasn't home when they arrived, John, my son-in-law, had it all hooked up, and in the place where my old one was. Really sneaky! I surely never expected that!

Then, with Christmas observance over, the year was soon to end, with all its memories tucked away!

Marjorie M. Beyersdorf

Marjorie with great-grandson, Pierson, 2013

2013

In 2013, the New Year's first "special event" was traveling to Dwayne and Nichole's farm to celebrate Dwayne's mom's birthday. January 7th is Mary's birthday, and she was by her son's farm. Again, we met in Stevens Point and went together, with Lanetta driving the rest of the way. We had the homemade German chocolate cake that is our family's favorite birthday cake. No candles though, we know we're getting older! We stayed for the afternoon milking, helping to milk the cows in their parlor. It was a fun-filled day!

January 9th was our annual farm co-operative meeting. This was the last meeting as Customer One Cooperative. The cooperative was unified together with a neighboring cooperative. No more meetings to go to for me!

Overall, January was a very cold month. There were several days I received calls to not to come in to work because of the low temperatures of twenty-five to thirty degrees below zero. *Burr, burr, burr!*

On February 11th, Richard called me. He wanted to know if I wanted to purchase the truck which he always drove to work. It was a Silverado pick-up truck, leased by the company he worked at, for the use of their employees. We had talked about the truck last year and I knew it would be good for me to have something with a four-wheel drive. My driveway has an upward slope and causes trouble in winter when slippery with a lot of snow. My little Saturn car doesn't make it up the hill! I said, "Yes, I would be interested in buying the truck."

The following evening, I received a phone call from Patti, Richards's wife. She informed me, "Rich is in the hospital, in intensive care." He had slipped on the ice at one of his farm stops, and his head took the brunt of it all!

I called in to work the next morning, and left early for the hospital. They were observing him closely for bleeding in the brain. All kinds of gadgets and graphs were hooked up to him. I am so thankful to say he stabilized without any abnormal signs. He was able to return home the third day after the accident. There would be no going to work for a while for him!

On February 20th, the truck financial arrangements were made; and five days later, Lanetta and Bob came up for a visit, bringing the truck, which was now mine. I shouldn't get stuck in the driveway now. My 'O-nine Chevy Silverado will take me right on up!

In spite of several days that were below zero chill factor in March, with each passing day, we would be getting closer to spring! Doing spring cleaning in the barn by Jeff, and in my home, was what kept me busy in between my job and daily routine work.

Easter was the last Sunday of the month. Preparations were being made for the family get-together. This year, I made a lot of chocolate éclairs, because several dozen were taken to work for the guys in my work area. They disappeared in short order.

"Surprise!" Lanetta called and said we were going to visit Jeremy and his family in Virginia. She had already purchased tickets for the both of us, leaving from Milwaukee airport on April 11th. I had never been to visit my son in Virginia. He had been living there for ten years already. Yes, a visit to his home was long overdue!

It was a great time together! Jeremy took us to Washington DC, where we saw quite a few historical sites. Eating out at different fancy restaurants was a treat, as were the delicious cook-outs of grilled salmon and steaks at his home. The good times together came to an end as we left from Reagan Airport on April 16th, with a destination back home, taking with us a lot of happy memories!

Coming back home from Virginia was like entering a different world. No green grass, flowers, nor warm weather here. It was several weeks before spring, with its warmer weather, finally came! The apple tree buds were responding to the rain and warmth, and not long after, they were blossoming. Almost simultaneously, the fragrance from the lilac trees filled the air.

Spring is the time for newborns, and wouldn't you know it? Jenny, one of the female donkeys, gave birth to a little male donkey on May 1st. He was the cutest little guy, and on Sunday, May 5th, a family from church came over after service for dinner to see him. Their son wanted him; he spent most of his time while he was here in the pen with the little guy. He said, "Now to wait till baby is able to leave its mom, and then he'll be mine!"

May 18th was the wedding day for my granddaughter, Shianne, and her beau, Brandon. I went to Lanetta's home, and changed clothes there for the ceremony, which was held at one o'clock in the afternoon.

The evening was spent with Lanetta and John, and the Community Firemen's Picnic was the next day. We ate at the picnic, visited with area folks, then left for Fishtail Inn to visit Lanetta's employer, who owned a greenhouse as well as his bar/grill. With a car full of flowers and plants, I headed for home.

The Family Reunion Comes to My House

Ten years have passed since our family hosted my mom's side of the family reunion. It was held on the farm then, in 2003. Rotating every ten years meant it was our turn again. Wanting the place to look nice, more flowers were planted than usual.

There were some things that needed to be done, so why not now, before the reunion? One was getting the two-car garage painted. It really needed a face lift! Mary came up on Saturday, July 6th and helped me paint. It took us two days. We kept at it, and it was totally finished by Sunday evening. Another project I wanted finished was staining the deck and steps. I tackled the project and had it done in a day and a half.

One more improvement, which I dreamed about having done, became a reality! Landscapers were contacted to come in to do the north and east sides of the house. These sides faced the front of the house and driveway, and were quite bare. They did an excellent job of planting perennials, bushes, and evergreen shrubs in a dug-out edged area, with chocolate-colored mulch as a base.

At the bottom of the driveway, there wasn't much room for parking. Jeff moved a stone pile and graded the area level. Before doing that, Jeff and our hired man tore down an old pump house which had no use. It was only an eyesore. A large dumpster was rented, and all the debris was put in there. One of Jeff's friends cut down some little poplar trees, which were close to the fence and had grown up by themselves. Last to be done, Jeff hauled several loads of gravel in and bladed it level. Wow! What a transformation; the place looked really great!

Lanetta came up and we went shopping together for a new grill, and whatever else was needed; things like paper cups, plates, chips, condiments, etc.

Mary came on Friday, two days before the reunion. She helped me clean the book shelves off upstairs. They weren't looking very orderly! On Saturday, Mary painted the outside basement door and the trim on the French doors in front of the house. Mike, my only nephew, came, and he, Mary, and I went to get table and chairs. After that, it was a good time of getting the last-minute food preparations ready.

Mary made potato salad, while baking was my job—rhubarb torte and brownies. Our one aunt and uncle who came earlier on Saturday were put to work; they cut up the fruit for our watermelon boat.

Finally, the big day was here! Relatives kept arriving until we had a total of at least forty-five people. My brother, Dick, and my son, Rich, were the grill masters, making the brats and hamburgers. The food was set out in front of the house on long tables where two little tents were set up, with table and chairs beneath them. Lanetta was the organizer, getting everything staged "just right". Everyone did their part. Lanetta, Patti, and Shannon brought food; and there was plenty for all to eat!

It was with gratefulness in my heart that I experienced how our family worked together in preparation for the reunion! As for the day itself, I was thankful for the delicious food, all being enjoyed as one big family together!

How great it was that my brother and Mary were with us at the reunion, and afterwards, stayed with me till noon on Thursday. One day while they were here, we attended our local county fair. We visited the State Academy Dairy Farm to view cows being milked by a robot. We went to a local cheese factory, grilled out at home, and just plain visited! I treasure these days with my brother. "These days" are always too few!

Marjorie M. Beyersdorf

Marjorie with her German Shepherd, Biggin, 2016

Biggin

At the beginning of a new month—August—I was reading the Buyers' Guide, when an advertisement intrigued me. A German Shepherd was for sale. Someday, I'd say, it would be nice to have a dog, and my choice would be a German Shepherd. Was this that "someday"?

I made a call to see if the dog was still available; the answer was yes, so I made arrangements to see him. On August 3rd, I drove about forty miles to take a look at the shepherd. He was outside, no one was around, and when I went up to him, I found he was friendly.

The owner drove in just then. He informed me "Biggin" was a registered German Shepherd. He was disciplined, trained, and had a friendly disposition. He even responded to his owner's commands in German. The dog took to me, and I to him. The owner said he'd hold him for me. I couldn't take him along right away, because a large dog house went with him and it was too big to load without extra help.

A week later, Jeff and a friend, Nate, and I went to get the doghouse and

Biggin. The following day, I was cleaning the car inside and out. That way, being outside, the dog could get acquainted with his new surroundings, with me being there.

I suddenly felt sick after cleaning the car, so I laid down. I wasn't feeling good on Sunday, either. Monday morning came and I called work, telling them I wasn't able to be at work. I would be going in to see the doctor. After taking tests, the doctor found there was an infection going on.

By this time, my right leg was real red, the apparent site of infection. On Tuesday morning, my leg was very swollen. I couldn't drive my stick-shift car, so Jeff took me in to the doctor again. I had to keep my leg elevated, with warm compresses on it, along with taking antibiotics. The doctor called it cellulitis, a skin infection. No work for me the whole month of August! The bright side was that this gave me a lot of bonding time with Biggin, my new dog!

Always Cared For

Lanetta and Bob paid me a surprise visit on August 26th. They picked beans and broccoli, doing the garden work for me. Lanetta vacuumed the house, took me to the credit union drive-through to deposit a check, and then they treated me to dinner at McDonalds. All just to get me out of the house, too!

September came, and with the leg healing, I was able to go back to work after having a total of three weeks off. The swelling was down, the redness was there yet, and I had to keep on applying a prescription salve until it cleared up.

On September 15th, friends from church that had been over for dinner in May came to get their son's long-awaited, little donkey. What a happy boy; his long wait was over!

September, too, was acquaintance time with my new great-grandchild, Henry. Eric and Janelle, the proud parents, visited awhile on the 22nd. Eric was finishing up his doctorate work at Harvard. He would be a full-fledged surgeon in July, when he finished—Dr. Stanelle!

Rich came two days before his birthday to deliver minerals to the farm. His favorite cake, angel food with pink frosting, was waiting for him! He took it home in the truck and saved it to have on his birthday.

At the end of September, I headed south for Lanetta's home so we could visit Bob together. He had knee surgery on the 16th of the month and was in a rehabilitation facility. Mary and Shannon came the same day to visit him. We stayed and watched the Badger game together in his room. Later that evening, we went to Lanetta and John's, and stayed there overnight.

The following day, we gals went shopping for a new toilet stool for Bob. The existing one had problems leaking, and also a high-rise one would be better for him. A unique get-well gift, I'd say! It was all completed, purchased, and installed before noon. John did the work of putting it in place.

There was a family get-together at Dairy Queen. We went to the rehabilitation center to pick up Bob, and Rich and Patti met us there, where we all enjoyed the noon meal together!

We returned back to the Rehab Center afterwards, checking Bob back in. Then on to Lanetta's place, and from there I left for home. Another full weekend!

Family Time No Stranger

October was garden clean-up time. I picked the last beans, and pulled the plants out by the roots, giving them to the donkeys, who really enjoyed eating them. I potted all the geraniums. Soon, they would be brought into the house before the frost came. A hard frost did come on October 16th.

Family time was no stranger amongst us. On October 21st, I met Lanetta and Bob in Stevens Point, and from there we drove to Dwayne and Nichole's farm. It really was an early Christmas visit. Lanetta was working two jobs before Christmas, so time didn't allow for her to visit later. We had lunch together, gifts and all. Not a normal Christmas visit, that's for sure!

On October 26th, I was in attendance at a party hosted by Kaye in De Pere, my cousin from my dad's side of the relation. Kaye's brother, Bob, and his wife from California were here visiting, so she took the opportunity to get everyone together for a visit!

October 30th, Jeff visited Florida. He came back on November 5th, bringing his friend, Monica, along with him. While Jeff was gone, I helped milk cows, morning and night, with the hired help. I also took care of the calves, and did miscellaneous small chores.

Mary and her daughter, Shannon, visited us on November 8th. Mary couldn't come for Thanksgiving this year, so they came up earlier. That evening, after the milking was finished, we all went out to eat—Jeff, Monica, Mary, Shannon, and myself.

On Saturday, the two gals did baking for me. Mary also made scalloped potatoes and veggies, for a "make ahead" early Thanksgiving dinner. That evening, Jeff and Monica joined us after the chores and milking were completed. The next day, Sunday, we all went out to eat for breakfast. In the afternoon, we went across the road to the Christmas tree farm to get evergreen boughs. Mary and Shannon wanted to take some back with them for Christmas trimmings. Early evening, they left for home.

The year was closing in fast! On November 21st, Jeremy, and one of his wife's cousins came for deer hunting season. They couldn't stay for Thanksgiving though, leaving within four days of being in Wisconsin.

On Thanksgiving Day, Evan, Christa, and their family came. Rich, Bob, Lanetta, Jeff, and I also enjoyed turkey with all the extras, and of course, the traditional potato dumplings. It wouldn't be Thanksgiving dinner without them!

Upon turning the calendar to December, I started getting thoughts together for my annual Christmas letter. It was completed earlier this year, on December 11th, much ahead of what was usually done.

On December 19th, I had a surprise visit by a former pastor of ours, Pastor Brunner. We had such a nice visit, catching up on a lot of happenings in our families, since we share the same grandchildren. The next day, a proverb from the Book of Proverbs in the Bible, Chapter 27, verse 1, came into play for me. "Boast not thyself of tomorrow, for thou knowest not what a day may bring forth."

Thou Knowest Not

It was Friday morning at work, and my job was cleaning the milk-house ceiling in the big parlor. After getting that completed, I went down to the bathroom before getting my next assignment. Not knowing the tile floor had just been washed, and was very slippery, my right foot slipped out from under me with my entire body weight landing on my right hip. It was a hard fall, and I hit the floor on my right side. I didn't get up right away and instead, motioned to a Mexican gal to get someone from the office.

They came and lifted me onto a chair. I had such faint feelings, like I was going to pass out! My employer and a co-worker carried me to my employer's truck and took me to the hospital.

In the emergency room, they put an IV into my hand, took all the vital readings, and got me ready for X-rays. After getting the results, which showed the femur bone at the hip was fractured, the ER doctor said I needed surgery. Three pins would be put in the area to hold the bone in place so it would heal together. The term they used was "hip pinning". So, I was admitted and taken up to my room.

Surgery was on the next day, at 3:30 in the afternoon. Friends from church came to visit me in the evening, and on Sunday, Amy and her son, Zack, came to visit. Amy was the gal who took me to the doctor and hospital four years previously, when I was thrown by a cow.

Really, how ironic! Now, I have three pins on each side, both sides identical. Now I know why I had taken care of the Christmas letters earlier. They wouldn't make it before Christmas if they weren't mailed out before the twentieth.

On Monday, my doctor said I could return home if someone was there with me. Early on Monday evening, a friend, Lisa, and her daughter came to take me home from the hospital. It was December 23rd, two days before Christmas. Mary, Shannon, and Gabe came up that same evening, not long after I arrived home from the hospital. They came to do some baking, and made preparations for our family get-together on Christmas Eve.

I didn't get a Christmas tree up early this year, so the girls brought a little artificial tree up from the basement, put trimmings with lights on, and it looked great! They kept busy into the night, but I went to bed early. It was so good to sleep in my own bed again!

Christmas Eve day, Rich and Patti, Lanetta and John, Bob, and Jeff and Monica all were here. Mary, Shannon, and Gabe were still here, too. We had a great time of exchanging gifts, with buffet food all day!

Another surprise visit came from Pastor Brunner. When he had visited me several days ago—in fact, the day before my accident—he asked me if the family was getting together? He hadn't seen Mary, Rich, Lanetta, and Bob for a long time. He said he might stop over, and so he did!

After Christmas Eve day, everyone but Mary had gone back home. Mary stayed with me a couple days and helped me take a shower and figure out how I could do it on my own when she wasn't here. I was thankful for a good neighbor, Jim, who lived across the road. He would bring the mail in and shovel off the back deck for me.

The visiting nurses from Aspirus came to the house once a week for three weeks. A gal from physical therapy came to help me do exercises, and show me how to do them correctly by myself.

The second to last day of December, Lanetta and Bob came up. Lanetta brought groceries for me. She did all the cleaning in the house, washed dishes, and watered all the plants and flowers. At the same time, she pulled off all the old, dry leaves and blossoms. She came up again on January 6th to take me to a doctor's appointment, the first doctor visit since surgery on December 21st.

Lanetta Helps Again

January 6th will be a day many people will remember as very, very cold, almost fifty degrees below the chill factor! After we were home from the doctor's appointment, Lanetta washed the kitchen floor, vacuumed the rugs, watered the plants again, and then she was on her way back home.

Lanetta's visits were many! On January 20th, she and Bob came up. She did all my laundry and cleaned again for me. They even moved the three-sectional davenport away from the wall, and vacuumed the entire area underneath. "Wow!" I said, "I have a jump on my spring cleaning!"

It was hard to believe it was one month since I had my surgery! Having this time off, with no work and a lot of sitting, gave me an opportunity to do some writing and work on my book.

Lanetta was here again on January 28th to take me to my second doctor's appointment. X-rays were taken, showing the healing was coming along really good! What a blessing my daughter, Lanetta has been! To always come up to help me and take me to my doctors' appointments, yet she lives over one hundred miles east of me, between the cities of Hilbert and Chilton in Calumet County.

I'm so thankful for all Jeff did for me. He would come over, at times, to feed the donkeys, bring milk over, and mail letters for me. Jim, a distant neighbor, would also stop in and bring hay for my donkeys. Certainly, it was a blessing to have all that help!

Super Bowl Sunday arrived! I sat through the whole game, watching the Seahawks take the victory. On the morning of February 5th, I had started my first physical therapy appointment at "Sport and Spine" in Wausau. From then on, it was every Monday, Wednesday, and Friday afternoon. I wasn't able to drive yet, so arrangements were made with Marathon Transportation to get me there and back.

By February 5th, I was starting to do a little more and more each day. I made cookie dough on the 10th of February, put it in the refrigerator overnight, and the following day rolled the dough out and made cut-outs using a heart cookie cutter. These became our sugar cookies for Valentine's Day. I gave some cookies away to Jeff and Monica, to the mailman, who would bring boxes to the front door (whatever didn't fit in my small mailbox), to the propane gas delivery man, and to visitors who came to visit me.

On February 19th, I walked out to the mailbox with my walker for the first time. Wow, there was a lot of snow! The winter had been very, very cold. Records were being set, with fifty-five days of below zero readings.

Lanetta and Bob came up on Monday, February 24th. She previously had called me, saying, "Mom you can't walk around in the grocery store very well yet; tell me what you need." She knows I like yogurt, was out of eggs and butter, along with several other items, all of which she brought for me. They shoveled off the back deck and steps; there was a lot of snow and ice on them. I always go out the front of the house, which has a smaller deck, with only one, more manageable step.

Back to Work

Tuesday, February 25th, was my first day back to work—two months and four days after surgery. I had restrictions; I was required to use my walker, could only work for four hours, and had to do sedentary work. I was given the task of shredding and tearing old records, and cleaning up three-ring binders for use again. I could handle that, and was thankful I could do something again! It even seemed strange to drive my car, after not being able to do so for several months!

On March 9th, I went back to church for the first time since my accident. On March 10th, I started driving myself to my physical therapy appointments. At work, I continued to shred old records. When I was finished with that, I put cow medical cards in order.

In mid-March, work began for me in the employer's horse arena. I polished bridles and saddles, working till noon, and then went directly from work to physical therapy.

March 18th was my first day back at Jeff's farm to feed the baby calves. Saturday, March 22nd was a day out together with Lanetta and Patti, Rich's wife. We drove together to attend a baby shower for Nichole, Dwayne's wife. It was held in the library hospitality room, in the small town of Plain, Wisconsin, about a three-hour drive from my home, and it made for one full day!

Back to my employment! Having finished all the saddles and bridles that needed polishing, I was given the job to wash down all the wooden areas on the individual horse stalls in the horse barn. After that, I started painting the black wrought iron on each stall. There was always something to do on the big farm!

Another birthday came, as it always does each year, and on my special day, March 27th, Rich came and took me out to eat. I continued to go to physical therapy three times a week, making the appointments after work in the afternoon.

On April 4th, it snowed an inch and a half. It was cold, just twenty degrees in the evening. Not long after, winter finally surrendered to spring, after having such a brutal, long cold season with a lot of snow.

On April 18th, Easter weekend, I was busy baking twelve dozen éclairs, a tradition at Easter time. I also made a springtime rainbow cake. On Saturday, Mary, Gabe, and Shannon came to the house at four o'clock. They helped put filling in the éclairs and frost them. They made salads, and we mixed and baked cinnamon sweet rolls until midnight!

Easter Sunday arrived, with Rich, Bob, Lanetta, and John coming up in Lanetta's new car. Rich grilled out rib eye steaks. The day went by fast, and all too soon everyone was on their way back home. On Monday, it was back to painting horse stalls!

I took Jeff and Monica to the airport on April 25th. They were flying out to Virginia to visit Jeremy, and planned on being gone for five days, back on Tuesday the 29th. The usual calf feeding was done by me. I and the hired help did the milking; he fed the cows, and cleaned the barn while Jeff was gone.

Ambitions run high when warmer weather is here! And the month of May was here. I did raking, only a little at a time, going slower, due to my injury. I picked up tree twigs and cleaned up the yard, which kept me busy the whole day.

At the big farm, I never knew what I'd be doing next! Having the horse stalls all painted, I was given the new job of hand sewing horse blankets. This work I could do while sitting, which was much easier for me.

On Mother's Day, Rich and Bob came over. Rich grilled out brats, and Monica brought salmon over to grill. It was a very nice day weather-wise, and we ate out on the back deck. Jeff wasn't feeling good, so he didn't join us.

My physical therapy appointments ended on May 12th. That concluded three full months, three times a week of therapy. That's a lot of exercise for the body! I had chiropractor visits, too, because my walking gait was not perfect, putting strain on my back. Usually, I'd go twice a week.

At work, throughout the month of May, I was kept busy hand sewing horse blankets. When the weather got warmer and dry outside, they had me painting gates, and posts and exterior doors.

Spring is always such an exciting time! All nature was bursting out in its greens. The lilac trees filled the yard with their beautiful fragrance. My neighbor rototilled the garden for me. It looked great and was ready to plant! The same day, grass was cut for the season's first time on our riding lawn mower. By Memorial Day, all the flowers and plants moved out of the house to enjoy nature's direct, full sunshine and rain.

The first weekend of June was rodeo time. My employer is big into horses, so to help get ready for the weekend, I cleaned their saddle room. Then afterwards, I went back to painting outside, weather permitting, and inside, when it was rainy and wet.

Life continued to flow; my job at the big farm, helping my son by feeding all the baby calves, yard work, baking, and routine work in the house. I was so thankful my body was healing, enabling me to do the things I love to do! Garden work for me is so enjoyable! I don't really consider it work!

On June 6th, I purchased plants and put them in their place in the garden. Lanetta came to visit on June 18th and we went shopping together. She stayed overnight with me, so she could visit with Jeremy and family who came for a visit the next day. Jeff had brought two apple trees for me; a life-time gift! Jeremy, Lanetta, and I planted them. Now, to wait for apples in a year or so!

On Sunday, June 22nd, Jeremy and his family would be driving back home, and I followed in my car. We all stopped in Wild Rose for a graduation party for my grandson, Eric. He had finished his doctorate, graduating from Harvard, with his title now officially Dr. Eric Stanelle, a surgeon specializing in surgery for pancreatic and liver cancers.

Let Go

Life for me had many sudden, unexpected moments! It was on June 25th that it had rained in the early morning, so for work I'd be painting inside. I punched in at eight o'clock, and started to sand a gate in preparation to paint it. But my employer came and said, "Don't do this one; welding must be done on it, so paint it after." He showed me a different gate to work on. Around ten o'clock he came down by me again. This time, he said, "Come down to the computer room."

Upon going there, I saw two papers on the counter, which I recognized right away. I had the copies at home—my reports from my doctor. With no advance notice given, I had been presented the dismissal document when I was taken away from painting a gate, and I hadn't even been half finished with it. The paper bluntly said, "Due to your doctor's restrictions, we no longer have work for you. June 25th will be the last day of employment for you."

It was so abrupt, and I thought it really strange! The doctor's restrictions hadn't changed; I had been working with the same restrictions from the previous accident. So, I ended my fourteen years of employment at the big farm that day. My daily schedule had always been very regimented; now, there would be some slack in my days.

The last Sunday in June was "Sundae on the Farm," an event I attended in Calumet County. It was an event held for city and urban folks, as well as other farm folks, to see what goes on at a dairy farm. I was a helper in buttering bread for cheese sandwiches in the food tent. Lanetta was one of the main organizers of the event. Mary, her daughter Shannon, and husband Gabe all helped in the food tent, too.

Sunday evening was spent by Lanetta's, and after an overnight stay, my return trip brought me home in late afternoon. In the yard around my house were trees with a lot of cracked, hanging limbs. There were two dead trees that needed to be taken down as well.

On July 3rd, a neighbor of mine drove in the yard. He said he would be glad to clean up the yard in trade for firewood. He cut logs out of the woods and had plenty of firewood to be cut up later. That was good news for me! No out-of-pocket expense to have it all done. He did a super job. I was so pleased with the way it all looked when he was finished!

In the middle of the month, I met Lanetta and Bob in Stevens Point. Together, we traveled to our grandson Dwayne's place to see the most recent great-grandchild, baby Pierson, who was born on May 16th. After visiting there, we drove further south to visit Mary. I arrived back home at ten-thirty that night after another "full day".

On July 17th, my son, Rich, a livestock production specialist employed by Land O' Lakes, delivered cow mineral to the farm. Being the noon hour, he, Jeff, and I went out to eat together in town. It was nice to have lunch with the two boys that day.

Usually our family reunion is held the last Sunday in July. This year, it was the first Sunday in August. I traveled to the reunion on Sunday morning, staying overnight with Lanetta, because the next day she was taking Bob and I to the State Fair in Milwaukee. What an interesting day it was! I was eager to go because I hadn't been to the State Fair in over twenty-five years, and wouldn't have gone by myself.

When I returned home, the garden was showering me with veggies! Sweet corn was ripening now. Every day I picked several dozen cobs of corn and put them by the road in a little wagon with a sign that read, "Corn for Sale". I froze a lot of green beans and broccoli, happy when all the garden work was up-to-date, because Mary wanted me to come down by her.

Not working on the big farm now, I left on Friday and stayed through Monday. We worked together in her kitchen, reorganizing things. After working on Monday, we went out to eat at a Chinese restaurant, and I left for home from there. Another weekend gone!

Now it was Jeff's turn. He left the following weekend to go up north. The usual work was mine to do: feeding all the calves still on the bottle, scraping down the cows, sweeping feed in to the cows, and cleaning up the milk house after milking was finished. Jeff had one person to do the milking, and another person to feed the cows and clean the barn.

Lanetta and Bob came up to visit me at the end of August. They brought me lots of cucumbers, as there were none planted in my garden. I made refrigerator pickles and cucumber salad. How good!

Projects

It was the beginning of a new month, September! I had dental work done, and my last visit to the chiropractor. The new month brought with it a lot of rain. On September 4th (won't forget that day), the barn flooded, all the way into the cow stalls, too. The basement in the house on the farm had water almost up to the top of the pool table, about three feet. Six inches of rain had come at one time! It took a few days to get everything cleaned up.

Some projects that need to be done get to be long overdue when living in the country with plenty to do. One project was the cleaning and sorting through my clothes closet. It took me two days to get it accomplished and in order, with all the colors grouped together, short sleeves with short sleeves, etc. It's keeping up with the small projects like this that make life simpler.

On September 11th, Jenny had her baby donkey. Then on September 15th, another baby donkey was born to Ginny. Two little playmates could be seen running up and down and around in their pasture area. They were so cute.

Having a lot of sweet corn, I invited a friend from church to come out. We cut corn off the cob, preparing it for freezing. The total day kept us busy. Together, we did up to thirty-six quart-size bags of corn. The following week, I prepared forty-five bags of corn to put in the freezer here for myself; plus, a lot of it was given to the family.

Another project, the double garage, was in need of work, cleaning and straightening out. Projects like this I could get to much easier now, with more hours at home, and no longer being employed. By the end of the September, the garage was spic and span! In the summer, with the warmer weather, I don't need to put the car in the garage. When the cold temperatures come and the snow falls, the car would go in the garage with ease.

Rich's birthday was September 29th, but this year, we celebrated it late, on October 5th. I met Lanetta, Bob, Rich, and Patti at a restaurant called Doc's Harley Davidson Place. We spent the afternoon looking at antiques, classic cars, and different kinds of animals there. It was an enjoyable day spent with family.

With garden season winding down, it was clean up time, and picking the last of the veggies. Then, on October 9th, I mowed the entire lawn for the last cutting of the season. There was still one mom donkey left to have her baby. It was born on October 23rd, and that made for three playmates!

At the end of the month, I had an appointment with my eye doctor. My distance vision seemed to be getting worse. I had cataracts present for a while already, and my doctor said, "They had been maturing rapidly." He advised me to have them removed. November 6th was set as the surgery date for the first eye.

Saturday, the first day of November, I went to Lanetta's to help her in preparation for a surprise birthday party for Bob and Rich, one party for them both. Rich had turned fifty, and Bob would be eighty on November 23rd. The party was held on Sunday, November 2nd at a supper club called Van Abel's in Hollandtown. It was a total surprise, planned with one against the other. Bob thought it was for his son, and Rich thought it was for his dad. The look on their faces was priceless. We had a sit-down, family-style dinner served for sixty-seven guests. It was a very memorable day; and another event successfully pulled off by my daughter, Lanetta.

November 6th was my eye surgery. Jeff took me to the clinic, and in a matter of few hours, I was finished. He picked me back up to return home. I couldn't believe how quick and easy it was! Yes, I can really see out of that eye now.

I had "heavy lifting" restrictions for about two weeks, the same restrictions as when I had my hip pinning. The following day I drove myself to the eye clinic to have a post-surgery check-up, which went well. I was really happy to be able to see clearly again.

Not quite a week later, our first big snowstorm came on November 11th, bringing with it six inches of snow. We had a nine below chill factor for several days.

Thanksgiving Day was soon approaching, and my thoughts turned to recipes and plans for the day. Many of the family came, and we had seventeen around the dining room table, all enjoying the traditional turkey, potato dumplings, several side dishes, pies, and all!

At the end of November, I put all the fall decorations away and got out the Christmas decorations so they would be ready to put up during the first week in December.

On December 5th, I had my other eye surgery. I am so thankful that all turned out so well. I no longer needed glasses for distance vision, only for reading. After my final eye check, the doctor said, "Your eyes turned out beautiful!" Shortly after the day of the second eye surgery, I started to feel really congested. It turned out I had a bout with bronchitis. I went to see my doctor to get some antibiotics, which were a great help to get better.

With Christmas around the corner, it meant I must get busy writing out my Christmas letter. Our neighbor from the Christmas tree farm across the road brought a Christmas tree to my door step. Not only one, but two, and told me to choose which one I wanted to keep. Once it was in the tree stand, I trimmed it right away that same evening!

On the next day, the 20th, I baked Christmas cookies, so I was all set for the family coming on Christmas Eve day. The family all came for a noon meal rather than staying late into the night. And as my daughter says, "We graze all day anyway!" Gifts were exchanged in the afternoon, and most everyone left in the early evening. I headed back over to the farm to help Jeff with the milking.

Now, it was a countdown to the final days of the year! I started to clean out files, making room for the "new"—2015. On New Year's Day, the filing cabinet was finished.

Challenges in 2015

The New Year started out with a trip to Fond du Lac on January 3rd, where my granddaughter, Sierra, was a candidate for the Wisconsin Junior Holstein Princess. (In December 2007, her sister, Shianne, had won the title.) There was an evening banquet held at the Holiday Inn. I was very happy to be present to see Sierra crowned as the 2015 Wisconsin Junior Holstein Princess. I stayed overnight at Lanetta's home, and that allowed us to attend church services together in the morning. After lunch, it was time for me to go home.

On January 12th, 2015, I got a phone call from one of my cousins, Leone, saying her mom had died in the early morning. She was ninety-five. January 16th meant another road trip, this time to Kaukauna for the memorial service for Aunt Ann King. She will be remembered as making the best divinity and so many other treats. My cousins, Kaye, Jim, Patti, and I sat together and enjoyed the luncheon after the service. It was good to see everyone.

Winter was very cold, with many below zero temperatures, although the months of January and February seemed to go by fast. I'd be getting taxes and paper work finished. I attended a ladies' weekly Bible study. There was writing to do; my time was always occupied!

There was extra work on the farm, including washing the entire milk pipeline by hand and getting it ready for inspection. Jeff was leaving on February 13th for a four-day vacation. I would spend more time on the farm then, helping out with the work. The day before Jeff left, I had a doctor's appointment, and on the way home, I received a phone call from my second cousin that her dad had died. February 15th was the memorial service for him, but I was unable to attend, due to Jeff's absence and all the farm work.

It always seemed like when Jeff would go away for a few days, additional challenges would occur. We had a cow calving with a twisted uterus, and had to call the veterinarian. Then a heifer got stuck in the headlocks in the feeding alley. We had to saw a pipe to get her out. The skid-steer quit, so a rented one had to be called for to be delivered. Yes, there was always something happening, but we managed it all! Plus, with all of those challenges, on the very same day, the electricity went out, which meant we couldn't milk till nine in the morning.

The end of February, Rich made his regular delivery of cow mineral to the farm. We had a brief visit together while we ate the dinner I had prepared for us.

The beginning of March, Lanetta, Bob, and I went to visit my grandson, Dwayne and his wife, Niki, and their little boy, Pierson. Niki's birthday was coming up in a few days, on March 6th. I baked her an early birthday treat—our family's favorite—German chocolate cake.

We had a few days of warmer temperatures, hinting that spring would be arriving soon. I took advantage of those days and started to rake the lawns.

March 15th was Lanetta's birthday, at which time she'd find a birthday card in her mailbox from me. We had decided that we would celebrate her birthday and mine on Easter Sunday, when the family would be together. We all would share in the delicious German chocolate cake!

Marjorie and her brother, Richard, 2015

Marjorie and her great-granddaughter, Charlee, 2016

Marjorie and Bob's grandchildren and great-grandchildren, Thanksgiving, 2015

My Story: Faith, Family, Farm

Three generations, 2016

Only Jesus

On March 27th, 2015, I turned 76 years old. On this day, in 1939, a baby girl was born to John and Hilda Lingle, and that was me! It's really something to realize that a timeline of 75 years had been lived—life with its joys and sorrows. In giving physical life to my seven children, whose lives I love and appreciate, my own life revolved around them; life with all of its uncertainties and insecurities.

I am confronted with the knowledge I am getting older. I've already crossed the Biblical line of "three score and ten" (70 years) as stated in Psalm 90:10. I don't feel old, but I am getting older.

Reflecting on the past, I am so thankful God has allowed me to live this life! His mercy, grace, longsuffering, and patience have been abundant. There was a time in my past that I tried to live a Christian life, to please God and even said to God, "Aren't you glad you got me to do Christian work?" Wrong!

I am so grateful that I came to know I don't live this life by myself. No one can live the Christian life on their own; not by self-effort, following religious rules, or striving in works. It's only Jesus who can live it through us. Jesus said, "I am the Vine, you are the branches. He that abideth in me, and I in Him, the same bringeth forth much fruit, for without Me, you can do nothing" (John 15:5).

Jesus is my joy in living! The joy of the Lord is my strength. I have learned not to let the business and distractions of life take away that joy. By faith, Jesus thru His Spirit within me dwells. And someday, that faith will become sight!

In my dining room hangs a homemade wooden frame with my inscription, which reads:

"Until I learned to trust, I did not learn to pray.
And I did not learn to fully trust, Until sorrow came my way.
Until I felt my weakness, His Strength, I never knew,
Nor dreamed till I was stricken, That He would see me through.
Who deepest drinks of sorrow, Drinks deepest too of Grace.
He sends the storm, so He Himself, Can be our hiding place.
His Heart that seeks our highest good, Knows well when things annoy.
We would not look towards Heaven, If earth held only joy."

My story has no ending. Hebrews 11:1 states, "Faith is the substance of things hoped for, the evidence of things unseen." Faith is trusting in advance, which will only make sense in reverse.

My Story: Faith, Family, Farm

Dear Reader,

As one who was born into a family that loved me, that love was suddenly snatched away. From that point on, my life was characterized by uncertainty, fear, and loneliness, unsure if anyone loved me. Life at many times appeared as a maze.

Throughout my past, I've come to know the One True God, who does love me. Looking in the rearview mirror of my life, God was always there, even though many times I didn't recognize Him. In John 4:10, it says, "Here is love, not that we loved God, but that He loved us, and sent His Son to be the Sacrifice for our sins." In John 4:19, it says, "We love him because He first loved us."

I've learned we don't break God's laws; rather we break ourselves over them. I praise God for His unconditional love and forgiveness, and I praise God and thank Him for my family, and for their love.

Herewith, I shall share my motto, which I put upon a brown paper grocery bag framed in a golden antique frame where I've hand-printed these words.

"In my bedroom hangs my motto, and its place is near the door,
So that it will remind me, God, no one else must be before.
Never do I leave the bedroom, I see the motto there, as it seems to say,
Have a word with God, Your Father, before you go upon your way.
When I'm dressing in the morning and I see it hanging there,
It reminds me of my duties which I need commit to Him in prayer.
Duties, burdens, troubles, sorrows, all may come to me this day.
How can I prepare to meet them? How, I ask, except to pray!
Ready, dressed to get a'goin with little time to spare, in prayer,
I place myself and all my goings in my Heavenly Father's care.
Nightly, too, the motto speaks when for sleep I do prepare.
Whispering its own dear message, First God, go to Him, and rest in prayer.
Yes, "God First", must be my motto, if I would succeed each day
in all my ways to prosper, then, about them I must pray!"

Do you ever wonder about God, and His Great Love? That He really does love you? Wonder no more!

In my Heavenly Father's Great and Everlasting Love,
Marjorie M. Beyersdorf
　　　　—To God, be all the Glory!—

Potato Dumplings
Stanelle family recipe

Ingredients

Potato Dumplings:
3 cups white potatoes, peeled, cooked, and put through a potato ricer
2 tsp salt
1 cup flour
1 egg (beaten)

Gravy:
1 pint of sour cream
½ cup of brown poultry drippings
1 TB of butter (salted, not margarine)
Pinch of salt

Directions

In a large bowl, mix all the ingredients for the potato dumplings until it is the consistency that you can make it into a (cookie) roll about 2 inches thick.

If it is sticky, add more flour and work it on a floured surface.

Slice off ¾ - 1 inch pieces, dropping the pieces into boiling water that has been salted. Simmer about 3-5 minutes, until the dumplings pop to the surface.

Stir once, so the dumplings won't stick to the bottom of the kettle.

When the dumplings float to the top, remove with a ladle and place into a colander to drain.

When completely drained, place in a serving bowl.

Next, take sour cream, salt, poultry drippings, and butter and combine in a small pot for the gravy. Heat the mixture slowly until hot on a low burner so the cream doesn't separate.

Pour the mixture over the dumplings and serve.

Note: Not enough flour added, and the dumplings will fall apart when boiled. Too much flour, and they will be too hard. (Even your garbage disposal won't be able to "eat" them.) It is trial be error until you feel you get the feel for the right amount of flour.

For a large family (12-15 people), use 15 pounds of potatoes, 12 beaten eggs and 12-13 cups of flour.

Acknowledgements

Thank you to Michael J. Guckenberg, the Vocational Rehabilitation Consultant, who spent time with me after my first accident. Mike, you ignited a spark within me to write this book.

Thank you to Cousin Jim Stanelle for his help in providing some of the photos for this book.

A big "thank you" to my editor, Brittiany Koren, and her team for putting up with all my hand-written pages, and doing the super work they did. Thank you to all of you, my friends, who prayed for me and with me for the book. A special thanks to Barb Schoenherr for all her input.

To God goes all the Glory! Who initially has laid it upon my heart to share my story, and His Working in my life, and drawing me to Himself. A daily relationship with my Heavenly Father, yes to Him goes all the Glory!

About the Author

Marjorie M. Beyersdorf lives in Wausau, Wisconsin and has spent her life caring for her family, farming, and working with cattle. She came to know the Lord through the many hardships she's had in life. She has won several awards for her hardworking ethics. She was runner-up for Wisconsin Farmwoman of the Year 1996, and in the same year, she also graduated from North Central Technical College for Farm Business Production Management. She continues to be active in feeding calves and assisting in the milking of the dairy herd on the home farm. She has seven children, ten grandchildren, and eighteen great-grandchildren. ***My Story: Faith, Family, Farm*** is Marjorie's first book. Visit www.writtendreams.com to learn more about her and her book.

www.ingramcontent.com/pod-product-compliance
Lightning Source LLC
Chambersburg PA
CBHW020616300426
44113CB00007B/670